STORIES FOR YOUNG CHILDREN

Warren Clarke

Text Copyright © 2024

Warren Clarke

All Rights Reserved

Table of Contents

THE EMPTY PALACE 1

THE CLOCKWORK SAILING SHIP 13

THE SILENT DRUM 22

THE WRONG DREAM 32

A LOVELY HEAD OF HAIR 39

A STARRY NIGHT 56

'LUCKY' 65

THE KING'S CROWN 73

THE TEACHER WHO LIKED TO SCOLD 82

THE SHINY KNIGHT 91

THE DOLL AND THE TOY SOLDIER 101

THE BOY WHO WANTED TO BE 109

THE WELL 118

THE GREAT MARVO 127

THE MOUSE THAT SLEPT IN A STOCKING 135

THE SWEET SHOP 146

OVER THE HILL 153

BOSSY BOOTS 160

THE FRISKY DOG 169

THE SNEEZE 177

SWAPS 182

THE EMPTY PALACE

On a distant hilltop in the land of Binangon stood a glass palace. Yes, a palace completely made of glass. It was a wonder of the world, in the view of the people in the village below. They would climb out of bed every morning and gasp at the sight of it as the sun's rays caused it to glitter and sparkle.

Yet something about it puzzled them. For palaces are where kings and queens live, and nobody could recall ever seeing a king or a queen. Some scratched their heads and *seemed* to remember a king who'd lived long ago. Some screwed up their faces and preferred to think it must have been a queen, for they were sure that no king had ever ruled the land of Binangon. Either way, none of the villagers argued about it till they were blue in the face, because they just didn't know.

Not even the palace guards did. They stood outside the entrance, holding their long spears, and they couldn't remember ever seeing a single member of the royal family. Neither they nor those who came to take their places when the guards were changed, which happened three times a day, were any more informed than the villagers.

A mystery, that's what it was, and Peter and Petra were determined to get to the bottom of it. They were brother and sister – twins, in fact, though you wouldn't have thought so to look at them. Peter was round-faced and fair-haired; Petra was oval-faced and dark-haired. Peter liked to think hard about things; Petra was rash and impulsive. Peter took the lead in most of their activities; Petra went along as if for the ride.

So Peter it was who decided that they must get inside the palace, since that was the only way to find out if a king or a queen was living there.

But how? How could they get in with so many guards watching the entrance? The guards didn't look very friendly, and they wouldn't want a couple of children trying to sneak past them. Some other way would have to be found.

As it turned out, it wasn't difficult at all. When they went looking round the rear of the palace, they came to the back door. It was made of glass, of course, but it wasn't locked and all they had to do was to push it open – which they did.

They walked in a little nervously, not knowing what to expect. But the room they entered was empty. It seemed to be the kitchen. If a cook had been there boiling some potatoes or slicing some vegetables, they would have known for certain. But there wasn't. So they went through a door into another room. It had a large glass dining table in the middle, with three glass chairs along each side and one glass chair at each end. Presumably, thought the children, the chairs at the end were for the king and the queen.

'They must have lots of children,' suggested Petra. She assumed the chairs along the sides were for them.

'Unless they're for lords and ladies,' said Peter.

They went on exploring the palace, passing from one room to another, but not once meeting anyone.

Then they entered a large hall. At one end of it stood two large glass thrones. Naturally, they couldn't miss the opportunity to sit on thrones belonging to a king and a queen, so they went and sat on them. It made them giggle to think they were doing it.

Beside the throne on which Peter was sitting was a small glass table, and on the table was a glass bell.

'Ring it and see what happens,' said Petra.

Peter picked it up and waggled it. A tinkly, glassy sound echoed round the hall. At first, that was all. Nothing else happened. Then they heard footsteps padding towards them and saw a very tall thin man with a sombre expression approaching them. He was clasping his hands together and looked as though he hadn't smiled for ten years or more. As he reached them he bowed his head slightly.

'Yes, Your Highness, what I can do for you?'

Being addressed as Your Highness made Peter look at Petra in surprise. They whispered together so the man couldn't hear them.

'We'd like some lemonade and a slice of chocolate cake, please. For each of us.'

'Yes, Your Highness.' The man gave another bow and padded back the way he had come.

'You shouldn't have said "please",' said Petra. 'Kings never say that. They give orders and people have to do as they're told.' She seemed certain about that, so Peter didn't disagree.

They didn't have to wait long, for presently the man returned with a much smaller man who was carrying a tray on which were two glasses of lemonade and two slices of cake on two small glass plates.

Both the men gave slight bows as Peter and Petra took their pop and cake. Then they left as the children gobbled the cake down before slurping in some of the pop. They would have preferred straws but they'd forgotten to ask for those.

Their appetite satisfied, they wondered what else they could do as king and queen. Peter said he'd rather like another slice of chocolate cake, and was about to ring the bell again when Petra said she'd like a ride in the royal coach.

'They're bound to have one. All kings and queens have royal coaches.'

So Peter rang the bell again. A few moments later, the tall thin man reappeared. He gave his now familiar bow, then said, 'Yes, Your Majesty. What can I do for you?'

'My queen would like a ride in the royal coach. Arrange it.' This time Toby had not used the word 'please'. He had issued an order which he expected the man to carry out promptly. And the man did.

'Immediately, Your Majesty.' Having said which, he went back the way he had come and left the hall.

'He said "Your Majesty" this time, not "Your Highness",' Petra pointed out. 'Strange, that. Still, I'm glad you didn't say "please" when you said I wanted a ride in the royal coach. See how quickly he obeyed you.'

Peter nodded. 'He had no choice. I'm the king.' Peter was getting used to having authority, and felt proud and important. So he started feeling impatient when the tall thin man didn't return for a few minutes. It seemed ages before he reappeared.

'The coach awaits Your Highness at the entrance to the palace,' he informed Peter with another bow.

'About time too,' snapped Peter, without thanking him.

He and Petra got up and made their way to the entrance. Petra was thrilled at the prospect of having a ride in a royal coach. Peter, feeling proud and important, tried to remain more dignified. But when he saw the coach, even he couldn't help feeling a sense of awe. It was made entirely of glass. Even the wheels weren't the wooden ones to be seen on ordinary royal coaches; they were of glass too.

Petra couldn't wait to climb inside. Peter held up his hand for her to wait till one of the royal attendants helped her. There were four attendants standing near by. One of them dutifully stepped forward to assist her. Then Peter too was helped up.

The seats on which they sat were made of glass and, truth to tell, they weren't too comfortable. But the horses were real. There were four of them, all white, and when the coachman cracked his whip, they started pulling the coach along. They had to travel downhill to reach the village, and when they did, the villagers gaped in astonishment at the two children sitting inside. Peter and Petra started waving to them, but most were too bewildered to wave back.

It wasn't long before the coach came to the house where Peter and Petra lived. Their mother was standing by the front door. At first she had seen only the coach approaching. But when she saw her two children inside – waving excitedly at her – she seemed to lose her senses.

'Why, it's Peter and Petra. They must have been king and queen all along, and I didn't know it. Just wait till their dad comes home from work. He will have a shock.'

The coach passed by, with the two children looking behind as their mother faded into the distance.

'We should have asked her if she wanted a ride,' said Petra. 'She is the Queen Mother, you know.'

'The King Mother as well,' Peter pointed out. 'I don't think she would have liked sitting on these glass seats, though. I'd rather have the chairs with cushions at home. Should we ask the coachman to take us to another country? We've never been abroad.'

Petra wasn't too keen on doing that. 'The people speak funny languages there. I bet they don't even understand each other half the time.'

So they didn't bother. They went into the countryside, had a good look at the sheep and the cows in the fields, and even waved at them. Then Peter gave the order to head back to the palace. For one thing, their bottoms had had quite enough of those glass seats.

They didn't reach the palace. As they came to their house again, a man was standing in the middle of the road, so the coachman had to bring the coach to a halt. The man was their father. He had a frown on his face with which they were only too familiar.

'What on earth do you think you're doing in that silly coach?' he demanded. 'Get out at once. I'm not having you two parading round in that, thinking you're better than everyone else. Off to bed with you. You're having no supper tonight.'

Crestfallen, Peter and Petra climbed out of the coach and hurried inside the house.

'And you,' said their father to the coachman. 'Be off with you.'

The coachman cracked his whip, and the horses pulled the coach away.

The two children didn't return to the palace – not the next day nor any other. They grew up and occasionally looked up the hill towards it, remembering when they had ventured inside.

It still seemed empty. And would remain so.

Till someone else went round to the rear, pushed open the back door and entered; then walked through into the large hall, sat on the throne and rang the bell.

The tinkly glass bell.

THE CLOCKWORK SAILING SHIP

Captain Curly stretched and yawned as he lay on his bunk in his cabin. He looked through the porthole by his head and saw some clouds floating past. Good – there was a wind to fill the sails and speed the ship along. Time to make a move, he thought. Time to roust his crew as well. But he didn't rush into it. Another five minutes wouldn't do any harm. He yawned again. Captain Curly did a lot of yawning. He never seemed to get enough sleep. That was what he liked to do more than anything   sleep. There was nothing else he really needed to do, except what he was about to do. In a minute or two, that is. But he did have to do it, and so, eventually, he got up and started dressing. He had to make himself presentable. After all, he was the captain, and captains – even lazy ones – were supposed to look smart in neatly pressed uniforms. He had a white one. Once he'd buttoned the jacket, he combed his curly hair and put his captain's hat on. Then he went out into the sunshine.

    It was very windy indeed. Just what was needed for a long voyage. And a sailing ship like his, with its two masts and numerous sails, thrived on long voyages. Reaching into his pocket, he pulled out a large golden key and went over to the main mast. There was a keyhole in the mast. Captain Curly inserted the key and turned it right round, not once but twice. Then he waited. He smiled as he thought of the sailors below jumping out of their hammocks and getting dressed. They'd soon be appearing, eager to get to work, unfurling the sails that weren't already billowing in the wind, scrubbing the deck and doing the other chores that sailors had to do. He liked to watch them, making sure they didn't do anything to sink the ship. Ha-ha! He always chuckled at that little joke. No fear of that while he had his beady eye on them.

Sure enough, a minute later, the sailors began to appear, one by one, and immediately took up their allotted positions. But not with enthusiasm. They looked miserable, whatever job they had to do. One started climbing a rope ladder up the main mast, followed by another. A third got a bucket of water and a scrubbing brush, then dropped to his knees and started scrubbing the deck as hard as he could. That was on the starboard side, while another sailor did the same on the port side. Captain Curly had no need to issue orders. The sailors followed their daily course of activities, climbing masts and unfurling sails or scrubbing the deck. Or keeping everything shipshape, as everything should be on sailing ships.

Seeing that the sailors were busy at their duties, Captain Curly set up a deck chair which he always kept handy, and sank into it. He closed his eyes and yawned again. He had a good crew, he had to admit. They never gave him any trouble. Just got on with their work. They wouldn't mind if he had a little nap.

Oh, wouldn't they just! The clockwork sailors may have had to do their chores once the key had been turned twice but that didn't stop them grumbling to each other. It was always the same. They had to do the work while their lazy captain dozed the day away. There was some muttering between them about doing something about it, but how could they mutiny? So long as the key was turned, they were stuck in the ruts they occupied – climbing the masts, unfurling the sails, scrubbing the decks. Even the men who steered the ship were. There were two of them who took it in turns. One was on duty during the day, the other at night. They were clockwork too. So, much as they would have liked to, they couldn't steer the ship onto some rocks and sink her. They had to follow the course they'd been set.

Thus the day passed, with the sailors working their fingers to the bone while Captain Curly snored away. That might have seemed funny to some people, but to the sailors it was insulting.

'If we could get our hands on that key,' suggested Hiram Birch, one of the cleverer sailors, 'we could throw it away. Maybe then –'

'How can we do that?' demanded another. 'It's not our job to touch it. We're only clockwork sailors who do what we're supposed to do.'

All this time, of course, the key was unwinding to where it was when Captain Curly first inserted it in the keyhole. It was the sailors' task to finish their work and return below before it got there. And being clockwork sailors they never failed to do so. Nor did they on this particular day. When Captain Curly woke from his rather long nap, they were already on their way down.

'Good work, lads,' he called after them. Then he went down to the captain's cabin, where his comfy bunk was waiting for him.

And soon he was snoring away.

The following day started off in the same way.

But not for long. For one thing, it was much windier than even on the previous day. A storm was brewing, with pitch-black clouds on the horizon. There was nothing unusual about a storm at sea; Captain Curly had often sailed his ship safely through them. But there was something else. Some of the sailors had got halfway up the masts, when they found their bodies starting to creak and slow down. Likewise, the sailors who had to scrub the decks managed to dip their brushes in the water, when they too creaked and slowed down.

After a while, none of them could move at all.

Captain Curly was just settling down in his deck chair when he realised that work had come to a standstill. At first he couldn't understand it.

'Come on, lads,' he urged. 'No idling on the job.'

But still no one moved. Captain Curly remembered turning the key twice – he'd never forgotten to do that. So why –

Suddenly it dawned on him. He hadn't oiled the mechanism for a few days. He jumped up. It was the fastest he'd moved for a long while. But the storm was approaching. He had to get the sailors working again before it was too late.

But where was the oil? Where did he keep it? He couldn't remember. He was so forgetful at times. Lazy and forgetful. It was because he was so lazy that he'd become so forgetful. He never had the need to remember anything – apart from turning the key round twice. And he couldn't forget that or he wouldn't be able to have a nap during the day.

Where did he keep the oil?

But now the storm had arrived and was tossing the ship this way and that. The fierce wind was attacking the sails as if it wanted to tear them from the masts. Captain Curly looked on with alarm. If he didn't get those sails furled up, there would soon be none left.

And just when he remembered where the oil was kept, one of the sails on the foremast started ripping. Lazy and forgetful he was, but when his ship was threatened with disaster Captain Curly was full of courage. He ran to the mast and started climbing the rope ladder to the sail. He intended to furl it up before it was torn away completely. His cap went flying off in the wind, but he ignored that and reached the sail just in time.

Well no, actually he didn't, because as he seized hold of it, the wind wrenched it from the mast and carried it away over the sea.

With Captain Curly clinging to it.

And he didn't come down for a long time. Over the sea and over the land. Right around the world he went, desperately holding on to the sail, till he landed safely somewhere.

Or didn't – and was never seen again.

No one knows either way

THE SILENT DRUM

There were three days to go before Christmas. Only three. Six-year-old Tommy Plumb was as excited as any child between the ages of three and ten would be. Some eleven- and twelve-year-olds too, no doubt. A few two-year-olds maybe. Not many of those would understand that Christmas meant presents. But Tommy did. And he'd been pestering his parents for weeks about the things he wanted. They listened patiently, amused at the never-ending list of rather expensive toys and gadgets he assumed would be heading his way.

'We'll see what we can do,' his mother would say. Or if it wasn't his mother, it was his father in a deeper voice.

Remembering the pleasure they'd had when looking forward to Christmas as children, they didn't begrudge their son the same. So when, having been to the cinema to see *Barry in Wonderland*, they passed Folcy's Toyshop, they smiled at each other as their son gawked at the toys in the window. Fortunately, the shop was closed at that time of night, so Tommy couldn't plead to be taken inside to choose something. (Well, he could, but it wouldn't have done any good.) And they grinned and chuckled as he begged them to buy one particular toy after another. That one, then that one, then a third and a fourth ... The model aeroplane, the building blocks, the train set, the little soldiers with rifles, a paint box ... it went on and on.

Till he saw the drum.

That was when his face took on an expression of pure joy.

He desperately wanted that drum. To bang and –

'You're not having that, so don't think it,' said his mother. 'I'm not having you going round the house banging that all day.'

So it seemed that a drum was out of the question. But his father recalled his own little drum when he was about the same age, and the fun he'd had making a racket with it. He saw no reason why Tommy couldn't go out in the garden and bang one. So the very next day, without telling his wife, he returned to the toyshop and asked the bespectacled woman behind the counter if she had a drum which didn't bang very loudly.

'Oh yes,' said the woman. 'We have the very thing. We have one that doesn't make a bang at all. Or any noise whatsoever.' She went and brought it to show him.

It was just like any other little drum, but when Mr Plumb gave it a whack with the drumstick, he found the woman was right: it didn't make any sound at all.

'Just the job,' he said. 'I'll take it.'

When he got back home, he made sure Tommy wasn't about before he took the drum in and showed it to his wife, explaining about the silence when he hit it with the drumstick. Mrs Plumb was very sceptical. She'd never heard of drums like that before. Mr Plumb was about to give her a demonstration when he heard Tommy coming in, so he very quickly had to hide it.

Nor did he get the chance to prove that the drum made no sound till Christmas Day arrived and Tommy could see what presents he had.

Naturally, the drum took pride of place. He immediately put the cord round his neck so that the drum hung down at his waist. Then he grasped the drumstick and started banging the drum.

Except that it didn't start banging.

There was dead silence. The drumstick was definitely connecting with the drum, but no sound came.

It didn't seem to bother Tommy. He was quite happy banging away even if it wasn't banging. His mother frowned. She wasn't sure she approved of this strange state of affairs. His father was tickled pink. He'd bought the drum, so he felt he'd contributed to his son's undoubted pleasure. Tommy hardly looked at his other presents. For now, he was content to concentrate on banging the drum. The silent drum.

Of course, when Mr Plumb went off to work again after the holiday, he didn't have to listen to it. But Mrs

Plumb did. And it wasn't long before all that silent banging began to irritate her. Tommy wasn't back at school yet, so he was at home all the time, and because it was cold at this time of year, he spent most of it indoors – banging away. It was all right for her husband to escape from it all, but she had to stay and endure it. No matter how many times she told Tommy to stop banging the drum, it wasn't long before he started again.

Bang, bang, bang!

Or rather: silence …

She complained to her next-door neighbour about it.

'I hope it's not disturbing you, Ivy,' she said. 'I know how annoying it is when there's someone living next door who makes a racket day and night.'

'Well, I must admit I think I've heard a bit of silence now and then, but it's not been too bad,' said Ivy, grumpily. 'I wouldn't want to make a fuss about it.'

Mrs Plumb thanked her for that – though Ivy's grumpiness suggested she wasn't being entirely honest and hated the banging as much as she herself did. Silence could be deafening, as everyone knew, and she would have been upset if she thought Ivy was suffering as a result of Tommy's lack of consideration.

After four days of Tommy's banging, she was at the end of her tether.

'If you don't stop banging that drum, I'll dump it in the bin,' she warned him.

That brought a sulk from Tommy. He couldn't bang the drum even more silently than he already did, so he had to stop altogether.

Reluctantly he did. But only for an hour. Then the urge to play another rat-a-tat-tat on his drum became too strong, even if it was a silent one.

Once Mrs Plumb heard that silent rat-a-tat-tat again, she flew into a rage. She grabbed the drum from Tommy, threw it on the ground and pushed her foot through it. Funnily enough it did make a banging sound when she did it.

Tommy was distraught and went off into a day-long sulk, refusing to speak to his mother whatever she said.

When Mr Plumb came home, he scolded his wife for what she'd done. She had to admit she'd lost her temper, and said she'd buy Tommy a new one – as long as it didn't bang like ordinary drums.

So the following day they went to the toyshop and asked for the same type of silent drum. Alas, the last one had gone. In fact, the one Mr Plumb had bought was the last one.

'But I have got a penny whistle that peep-peeps silently when you blow on it,' the same bespectacled woman said.

Mr and Mrs Plumb looked at Tommy to see what he thought of that. He didn't seem to mind, so they bought it.

And from then on, Tommy blew on his penny whistle morning and night, and it didn't make a sound.

But it drove Mr Plumb mad. Once he'd got home from work, the last thing he wanted to hear was a penny whistle going 'peep peep', even if it was a silent 'peep peep'.

'Give it a rest, Tommy. Please,' he begged. And for an hour or so Tommy did. But then he got the urge again and would raise the whistle to his lips and start blowing again. Again and Again.

But then something strange happened. His whistle disappeared. Tommy looked everywhere but couldn't find it.

'You've not lost it, have you, Tommy?' his father asked in an innocent tone of voice. 'That was very careless. If you can't keep an eye on things like that, you'd better not have them. Go and watch some television instead.'

So Tommy did. But all the talking on the television got on his nerves. How he wished it was as silent as the drum and that whistle.

THE WRONG DREAM

Ellie had learnt all about dreams and nightmares in her six years of sleeping night after night since she was born. She had dreamt pleasantly of furry animals and being at the seaside. She'd woken crying or screaming after having a nightmare of being chased by monsters or of trying to escape from a burning house. She had got to the point of wondering each night whether she'd have a dream *or* a nightmare. She didn't like being kept in suspense. It would be nice to know beforehand in order to prepare herself for the worst.

    But that, of course, couldn't happen, so she had got into the habit of crossing her fingers when she climbed into bed. Doing that was supposed to give a person good luck. Well, it didn't give her any. She now knew from experience that it was a waste of time and very silly. All she could do as she waited to doze off was hope for the best. She did repeat to herself, 'Dream, please. Dream, please', as if doing so might help to avoid a nightmare. But even that proved useless. A nightmare was just as likely to come to torment her as a pleasant dream was to make her smile.

One morning, however, when she woke up, it was dream she'd had which tormented her. Quite apart from finding it difficult to remember all of it – which is always the case with dreams – she was puzzled by it. She'd dreamt she was a lion who chased after people, wanting to eat them – with a huge mouth and large teeth.

She shouldn't have dreams like that, she thought. Lions should have them. For one thing, she liked her mouth and teeth as they were. She didn't want them any bigger – and certainly not teeth that size. She'd look so ugly with them like that. And the way she terrified the people in her dream. She wouldn't have wanted to eat them as a little girl. Why would she want to as a lion? She did chuckle, though, at how they had run away for dear life. That was funny. She wouldn't have minded being able to make them do that as a little girl.

Even so, she thought there was something wrong about the dream. She couldn't imagine a lion having a dream in which it was a little girl who went to school and sat in the classroom with the other children. She reckoned having a dream like that would give the lion just as much a shock as she'd had at having her dream. She assumed it was the same for all animals. Imagine an elephant having a dream in which it was a frog, or a snake having a dream in which it was a crocodile. They'd be a bit confused, to say the least.

On the other hand, it could have been worse. She could have dreamt she was a spider – ugh! Or a worm – UGH! No, being a lion wasn't too bad when she thought of what she might have been.

On the other hand again, she didn't want to *keep* dreaming of being a lion. And for a while that's what she did. The very next night, she dreamt of being a lion in a zoo, sulkily gazing out of its cage at the people gazing in. The night after that, she was a lion playing with its cubs in the wild. And then … she was a lion roaring with all its might at something or somebody. The trouble was, she couldn't remember all of her dream and exactly what she was roaring at. She racked her brains, trying to see in her mind's eye what it was. But dreams are hard to recall in every detail, and she couldn't.

She told her mother of how she kept dreaming of being a lion.

'Oh, don't worry,' said her mother, giving her a comforting hug. 'Dreams are only dreams. They're nothing to worry about. Imagine having a nightmare instead and being chased by a lion who wants to gobble you up. Better you do the gobbling than being gobbled yourself.'

That made sense, Ellie supposed – though she wished her mother wouldn't talk to her as if she was a very very little girl.

Still, it was hard not to worry about the dreams she'd been having. There was something about being a lion which troubled her. And when would they stop? Would she keep having them for the rest of her life? She wouldn't like that at all. At least, she didn't think so. That her whole life might be taken over by such dreams was disturbing. Even she understood that at only six years of age.

So she did wish they'd stop. If she only knew how to have other dreams instead, what a relief it would be.

Then, one day, when she was in the park and had just been on the swings, a large dog saw her. For some time it had been running after a ball thrown here and there by its owner. But it seemed to have got bored with that, and now that it had fixed its eyes on Ellie it turned its attention to her and started bounding towards her – as if like a lion it wanted to gobble her up. And it barked nastily. Ellie froze. She was frightened – of course she was.

But only for a second or two. For then something inside her started to rise. It was a feeling of some sort, an impulse to gather her forces and do what she had to do before it was too late. Her chest swelled. Her mouth opened wide – it really was huge now. And she roared.

Ro-o-o-o-o-o-o-o-o-A-RRR!!!!

Roared like a lion. How loud it sounded in the park. Everyone looked round in fear of seeing a lion on the loose. But all they saw was a little girl with a roar issuing from her huge, lion-like mouth.

So did the dog, which stopped in its tracks just a few yards away from Ellie. As far as it was concerned, only lions roared like that, and as big as the dog was, it had no desire to test itself against a lion. So it turned and bolted, leaving its owner calling after it to no avail.

And from that moment on, Ellie never had another dream about being a lion. She had been a lion. Once she had been what she dreamed of being, she didn't have to dream of it any more.

A LOVELY HEAD OF HAIR

Karen was blessed. She had the loveliest head of hair in the whole school. It was blond, as smooth as silk and usually hung loosely to her shoulders, curling inside. But even if her mother braided it in pigtails, it was still the loveliest hair in the school. And even if she had it in a ponytail it was still the loveliest. Whatever style she adopted, none of the other girls had hair which was even close to being as lovely.

And Karen never let them forget it.

Whenever she entered the classroom she would shake her head very slightly so that her hair started swinging gently back and forth. Any other girl would have had to shake her head like mad to get her hair to move at all, but so soft was Karen's that even the faintest of breezes would set it in motion.

    Naturally, Karen wasn't very popular. She was just too conceited for her own good.

    But she didn't care. As long as she had the loveliest hair in the school, she was perfectly content. She didn't mind at all that she had no friends to play with. Staying in the house and combing her hair in front of the mirror was to her just as pleasant a way to pass the time. That and going for picnics on Sundays with her parents. They usually chose a spot in the country near a river, where they would spread a large blanket on the grass and eat their sandwiches and cake on it while enjoying the view. On one particular day, however, Karen's father drove down a path into a wood. He couldn't go very far down it as the path narrowed far too much for a car. So they got out their blanket and their hamper, and were soon eating sandwiches and cake surrounded by trees. Then, while her parents had a snooze, Karen said she was going to pick some flowers. What she had in mind was to link the flowers together in a kind of crown, so she could put it on her head and make her hair look even lovelier.

'Don't wander too far,' her mother cautioned. 'We wouldn't want you to get lost.'

Karen had no intention of getting lost, so she thought it a very silly thing to say. She skipped away to where she could see some flowers through the trees. They were only yellow daisies. Karen was used to making daisy chains and putting them on her hair, so she went a bit further through the trees, searching for flowers of a different colour. Red ones, she hoped. Or blue ones. As long as she could link them together, she didn't mind too much – though she wouldn't have wanted them to look lovelier than her hair. That would have been to defeat the whole purpose.

Soon she had gone further than her mother would have liked. But it was worth it, because there in the distance she made out a cluster of red flowers. She hurried over to it, and started picking them one by one very carefully. She had to make sure the stems were long enough so she could push one through another and make a chain with them. She was concentrating so much that she didn't hear footsteps coming towards her.

It was only when she felt a shadow over her that she looked up – and saw a scrawny little woman with a walking stick. She was wearing full-length rag-like clothes, had a bent back and a large hooked nose, and her face was furrowed with lines of old age. Some of her teeth were missing, and most of those still present were black.

Karen could see them because the woman was leering at her.

'Hello, dearie. Picking some of my flowers, are you?' she croaked.

Her flowers. Had the woman actually said that? They were flowers growing in a wood. Why should they be *her* flowers? That didn't seem right at all.

'These are flowers growing wild,' she retorted. 'They don't belong to you. If I want to pick them, I will.'

'Oh, I'm not trying to stop you, dearie. If you want to pick some of my flowers to put in your lovely hair, by all means go ahead. I don't think I've ever seen such a lovely head of hair.'

Karen didn't understand how the woman could know she wanted to put them in her hair. But it was nice of her to admit how lovely it was.

'I'd rather like a head of hair like that myself,' the woman said. And for the first time, Karen turned her attention to the woman's hair. Her eyes almost popped out in disgust. The woman's head of hair was ugly. It was grey and dry, and seemed to be tied in knots which would take a lot of untying. 'You wouldn't let me have your hair for those flowers you're picking, would you?' the woman asked.

It was a startling suggestion. But much less so than the woman's next remark.

'You can have mine in exchange. I'll cut your hair off, you cut mine off, and we'll swap. How about it? Do you want those flowers or not?'

Karen found herself tongue-tied for about ten seconds. It was such a ridiculous proposal that she thought the woman must be mad. The idea that she would swap her lovely hair for the woman's ... bundle of knots ... was ridiculous. She stood up with some of the red flowers in her hand.

'I do and I'm taking them. But I wouldn't swap my lovely hair for your ugly hair for any price, you stupid old woman.' Having said which, she turned and ran back to her parents.

The old woman watched her go. A cruel, bitter smile appeared on her face. And she started muttering to herself.

> Little girls who like their flowers
> mustn't think they can pick them for free;
> for if they take them when they shouldn't,
> their lovely hair may pay the price of the fee.

It seemed to be a poem because of the rhyme at the end. But if the woman was a witch – which was a distinct possibility – and what she had uttered was a witch's spell, it probably didn't matter whether it rhymed or not. Karen could expect something very nasty to happen to her.

Clutching the red flowers, she ran back through the trees to her parents, who were just then rousing from their nap.

Since it was time to go home, it wasn't long before they'd packed their stuff into the car boot and were on their way. While her father was driving, Karen sat in the back, trying to link the red flowers together. The stems were long enough, but for some reason she couldn't get them through one another. Eventually, in a fit of impatience, she opened the window and threw them out. She'd stick to daisies in future.

That evening was when Karen's hair had its weekly wash. Karen always let her mother do it as she made such a lovely job of it. So she bowed her head over the sink as her mother poured water over it, then closed her eyes as the usual shampoo was rubbed into it and suds were formed which might have got into them. Her mother finished rubbing, then let the shampoo take an effect on the hair before she started rinsing the suds away.

Till it was all gone.

Then she looked in horror at the result.

Karen's hair had turned purple.

Karen still had her eyes shut, but now that the suds had been cleared she opened them.

The scream that issued from her mouth was so piercing that it brought her father rushing upstairs to see what had happened. His mouth dropped when he saw Karen's hair, but nothing came out of it.

Karen was half blubbing and half demanding to know what had happened. Her mother didn't know.

'I've used the same shampoo.' She looked at the bottle to make sure, but yes, it was the same. 'It must have been something already in your hair which caused it.' That didn't sound convincing even to her, but she was too perplexed to explain it any other way.

'Wash it again,' pleaded the tearful Karen.

'Do you want me to do it?' her father asked his wife. He meant well, but to his wife it was infuriating.

'No, I don't want you to do it,' she snapped. 'I've washed my daughter's hair enough times to know how to do it, thank you very much.'

Her husband thought it best to retreat. He went downstairs again, pondering the mystery of Karen's hair and trying his best to solve it – which he couldn't.

Karen's mother poured some shampoo on Karen's hair again. Then she rubbed and rubbed – more so than she usually did, in the hope that she'd rub the purple away,

And she did. When she rinsed the suds off, the purple had gurgled down the plughole.

But Karen's hair was now green – and a bright green at that.

Another scream from Karen brought her father running back up the stairs again, two steps at a time.

'Wash it again,' sobbed Karen.

But her mother couldn't. She'd been so determined to wash the purple away that she'd used up all the shampoo. The bottle was empty. Karen was inconsolable. She blamed her mother for spoiling her hair and blamed her father for not stopping her.

Then she remembered the ugly old woman in the wood. A witch – she had to be.

Karen told her parents all about her and how she had wanted to cut her hair off.

'Oh, there's no such thing as witches,' scoffed her mother. 'That's just a superstition. She was just a silly old woman who lives alone and has gone a bit funny in the head. Isn't that right, Albert?'

Her husband agreed, but only because he didn't want to frighten Karen. Witches did exist, as far as he was concerned, and could cast spells and –

He didn't like to think what it might mean for Karen.

In fact, it meant a sleepless night, tossing and turning in bed because of the green head of hair on the pillow. She couldn't get it out of her mind.

The following morning, of course, she had to go to school. She begged with her mother not to send her as she thought the other children would make fun of her.

'We have to send you unless you're poorly,' her mother said. 'Otherwise we could get into trouble with the police. Don't worry about your hair. Lots of people have funny-coloured hair these days.'

'I don't want funny-coloured hair. I want my lovely hair back.'

'You go to school and I'll buy another bottle of shampoo and wash your hair again when you come home.'

So Karen went to school with the hood on her coat over her head. None of the other children paid any attention at first; they'd seen quite enough of Karen's lovely hair. But when she was sitting in the classroom and the teacher told her to put her hood down – what a shock everyone had.

And what a shock Karen had … for not everyone poked fun at her. One or two of her classmates thought her green hair looked terrific – far better, they said, than when it was the other colour. That did something to ease Karen's peace of mind, but not entirely. She still wanted her lovely hair back. And there were children who did make fun of the green colour. The teacher didn't like to make things worse for Karen, so she said nothing about it and went on with her teaching as normal.

At lunchtime Karen rushed home. Her mother had bought another bottle of shampoo, and Karen insisted she wash her hair before they had their sandwiches. They went upstairs to the bathroom and Karen bowed her head over the sink, desperately hoping that this time she'd get her lovely hair back.

Her mother wet the hair, then poured some shampoo over it.

And rubbed and rubbed.

Then rubbed and rubbed some more.

Karen's hair was a mass of soapy suds – which then her mother rinsed away.

The green disappeared down the plughole … but left a head of black-and-white striped hair, exactly like a zebra's body.

If Karen's father had been at home, her anguished scream would have brought him dashing up the stairs once again. But he was at work a few miles away. It was a wonder he didn't hear it there and come dashing home. But he didn't.

'Wash it again,' begged Karen.

'I don't think it will do any good,' said her mother. 'There must be something wrong with you. I'd better phone the doctor and arrange an appointment. So she did, but couldn't arrange one for another week. So Karen had to go back to school with her zebra-like hair.

And now virtually all the children thought it was great. They wanted their hair to be like that. They pleaded with Karen to tell them how it was done … what shampoo she used … or was there a special dye one could buy? So Karen told them about the ugly old woman in the wood. A witch, she insisted. She had cast a spell on her because she was picking flowers which the witch claimed belonged to her.

Once they'd learnt how to get hair like Karen's, many of the children couldn't rest till they too had gone to the wood and picked some flowers so the witch would cast a spell on them. Most of them went without their parents, pedalling there on their little bikes. But the witch hated children, and when she saw so many coming to pester her, she left the wood and was never seen again.

So the children didn't have a spell cast on them. They were stuck with the same coloured hair they'd always had, till their parents allowed them much later in life to dye it in purple or green or black and white stripes.

It was different for Karen. The witch hadn't removed the spell on her, so whenever her mother washed it, a different colour emerged when the suds were rinsed away. It happened so many times that some colours returned more than once.

But one colour never came back.

The blond colour, when Karen really had a lovely head of hair.

A STARRY NIGHT

Danny lived on a farm in the countryside. The nearest school was three miles away, so on most days he would get his bike out and cycle there. In bad weather his mother drove him there in the car. When he wasn't at school, he usually had to help his father on the farm. He was only eight, so he wasn't given too much to do or anything that required immense strength, and for the most part he enjoyed the chores. He wanted to be a farmer when he grew up, and he knew he had a lot to learn if he was going to be a good one.

The worst thing about living where he did was that during the holidays he had no one to play with. So when he finished the jobs he'd been given, he was rather at loose ends. He wasn't particularly studious, and didn't want to spend his time reading books to help him with his schoolwork. It was holiday time, which meant no school and no schoolwork.

Sometimes he would climb a ladder to the top of a haystack in one of the fields and gaze up at sky. He'd watch the clouds go drifting past and wonder what it would be like to sit on one and go floating round the world, peering down at the people below. He had never been in an aeroplane, and, frankly, he decided he'd rather sit on a cloud and fly that way. It wouldn't be as noisy, for one thing.

One fine evening, when darkness had fallen, the moon and the stars were out, shining and twinkling brightly. The sky seemed radiant with the glow they cast. The black had been replaced by a dark blue. There was no street lighting in the countryside, so the illumination from the sky was all that there was.

Suddenly Danny had an idea. He wondered what it would be like to spend the night on the haystack under the stars. He could sleep there. His parent wouldn't mind, surely. So he went and asked them. They didn't mind. He wouldn't be in any danger, and as long as he was well wrapped up he shouldn't feel too cold. They never treated him like a namby-pamby. He was a farmer's son and had to be tough for the life he would lead in the years to come.

So, wearing a thick pullover and a coat, he went and climbed the ladder to the top of the haystack. He had a blanket and a small cushion, and was soon lying comfortably on the hay, gazing up at the thousands of stars. Thousands and thousands, it seemed, as his eyes got used to picking out the fainter ones. It was a wondrous sight, with the man in the moon, it seemed, returning his gaze.

He had been there for an hour and was almost dozing off, when a star fell from the sky. Danny had seen shooting stars now and then, but this was different. It didn't sweep across the sky. Nor did it flutter down like a snowflake. It simply dropped straight down and landed in the field near the haystack.

Danny sat up and looked towards it. That shouldn't have happened, he thought. He slithered down the ladder and went for a closer look. It wasn't as big as he'd assumed. And it wasn't twinkling. It was a dull white. It looked much better in the sky. Best put it back there, he decided. He knew his dad kept a hammer and some nails in the barn, so he dashed over to it, squeezed between the two large doors and went looking for the bag in which the tools were kept. Soon he was hurrying back to the star, with the hammer and four nails in his hand. Gingerly, he picked up the star. He wasn't sure how fragile it was and he didn't want it crumbling to pieces at his touch. To his relief it didn't. He carried it over to the ladder and started climbing.

The more he climbed, the taller the ladder seemed to be. He went up and up because the ladder did as well. The higher the ladder went, the higher he climbed, till he'd left the haystack a long way below.

He began to feel a bit scared of being at such a height. One slip and he could plunge to the ground. Best put the star just here, he decided. So he took hold of the hammer in a firm grip, placed a nail against the star and started banging it into the sky. He had to bang really hard as the nail wasn't going in so easily.

Bang! Bang! Bang!

He was making a dreadful racket.

'Oy! You there. What do you think you're doing, making such a noise?' It was the man in the moon, which was shining brightly a short distance away. 'I come out here for a bit of peace and quiet at night, and I have to listen to you. Give it a rest.'

'I've got to put this star back,' explained Danny. 'It fell from the sky and wasn't twinkling very much on the ground.'

'If it fell from the sky, it's because it had to fall from the sky,' the man in the moon insisted. 'Just mind your own business and put it back where you found it.'

'I'm putting it back where it belongs, and that's in the sky, not on the ground,' said Danny in a rather pompous tone, then went on banging with the hammer.

Bang! Bang! Bang!

Bang! Bang! Bang!

'Such impertinence,' grumbled the crotchety man in the moon. 'I'm not hanging round here to listen to that.'

So he floated away … all the way, in fact, to Mars, and became a moon there.

Danny hardly noticed he'd gone. He finished tacking the star into the sky, then slithered all the way down to the haystack. It was more fun going down than climbing up, that's for sure.

He lay down on the hay, pulled the blanket over him and gazed up at the stars. He could see the one he'd put there. It was twinkling again. He'd done a good job, he told himself.

Then he fell asleep.

But what a commotion in the morning! People converged on the farm from all around. They'd seen the moon floating away, and when they gaped more closely at what was happening, they'd spotted Danny on the ladder banging the star in the sky. Putting two and two together, they realised that the man in the moon wouldn't have liked all that noise, so, naturally, they blamed Danny for annoying him so much that they no longer had a moon to look at.

'It's your fault,' they scolded him. 'You interfering busybody.'

Danny tried to excuse himself by saying he was putting a star back in place, but it did no good. The moon was gone.

'I'm sorry,' he said, realising how upset everyone was.

'It's not us you should apologise to,' came the response. 'It's the man in the moon. He might come back if you do.'

So the very next night, when darkness fell, Danny went out into the fields and shouted out into the sky, 'I'M SORRY! I'M SORRY!!! I AM SORRREEEEEE!!!!!'

But to no avail. The man in the moon was so far away now that he couldn't hear him.

Or he didn't want to.

Some people are like that.

So the moon never came back … though anyone living on Mars could now enjoy the sight of it every evening, shining more brightly than it ever had before.

'LUCKY'

Lucky wasn't his real name. It was his nickname, foisted on him by friends of his who had a strange sense of humour. It wasn't because he himself was lucky. It wasn't because he touched other people with his hand and made them lucky. It was because whenever he touched anyone – or they touched him – something very bad would happen to them shortly afterwards. But not to him. Once his friends became aware of this curious quirk, what else could they do but call him 'Lucky'?

He found it quite amusing. Touching himself seemed to have no effect. He would shake his own hand to see what happened – and nothing did. He was immune to himself – that's what people said. So he had nothing to worry about. If he and another person came into physical contact, the other person had to watch out: a terrible accident might be in the offing.

A perfect example was what happened to a classmate of his. They had an argument over football and started pushing each other. They were soon stopped by a teacher, but no sooner had they gone their separate ways than the other boy tripped up, fell flat on his face and broke his nose. The teacher who had pulled them apart cycled to and from school every day. On his way home later, he had five punctures in the two miles he had to travel. That was why he decided to buy himself a car, which cost a lot of money – more than he could afford, in fact. So from then on he cut the cost on other things, eating only one meal a day for two years and cancelling his subscription to *Superman*, a comic he'd been collecting since he was a boy himself.

Then there was Audrey, a little girl who lived next door. She had just started kindergarten, and Lucky often had a bit of fun chasing her. When he caught her, her fate was sealed. Or rather her doll's was. For within an hour, one of its arms fell off and couldn't be repaired. That made her cry … and cry and cry, till her parents bought her a new doll – whose two arms both fell off after Lucky had chased and caught her again. She didn't cry this time. She threw the doll at her mother for buying such a cheap one. The doll hit her mother in the face and gave her a black eye.

Once Lucky got used to giving people bad luck, he did more than find it amusing – he went out of his way to do it. He even tormented his parents, Mr and Mrs Jessop, scaring them by deliberately approaching them without actually touching them. His mother would serve him his dinner by placing his meal on the table while insisting he stand well away till she'd done it. Then she said he could sit down and tuck in.

But in a small house like the Jessop's it was only a matter of time before it happened. Mr Jessop was going off to work one morning while Lucky was setting off for school – and their bodies touched in the hallway. Mr Jessop pretended not to have noticed and drove off in his car. He figured that if he didn't admit to himself that contact had occurred, any bad luck he might have had wouldn't happen.

He must have been thinking that when his car bumped into the back of a police car. Two policemen got out and came to speak to him. They weren't best pleased. They tested him to see if he'd been drinking, then took him off to the police station, where he had to face a lot of questions. They finally let him go after an hour, so he arrived late at work. His boss was annoyed at such timekeeping, especially when he learned that Mr Jessop had been arrested.

'Let that be the last time, Jessop. I can't have criminals working here. If it becomes a habit, you'll be looking for another job.'

When Mr Jessop got home and told his wife what had happened, Lucky was listening. He suppressed a snigger till he went upstairs to his room. He thought it great fun to give people bad luck.

And so his life went on. He loved to shake the hands of people to see what would happen to them later. A man who was keen to watch England play a soccer match against Germany hurried home to do so, only to find that his television broke down as the players came out. A woman's hat blew off down the road after she'd pushed past Lucky coming out of a shop. A man was drenched with water squirting off the road as a car passed. A woman, rushing to catch a train, caught the wrong one and ended up in Manchester instead of Cardiff. A thief who had stolen a purse from a woman's handbag dropped it but didn't realise till he got home and wanted to count the money he hoped would be inside ...

The bad luck never seemed to end for one person or another; it continued for years. And since Lucky was now held responsible for all of it, he was avoided by everyone. He didn't mind. He rather liked the power he seemed to have over other people.

But then an uncle came to visit. It was one he hadn't seen for years. At first he thought the uncle had stayed away because of his reputation. But the uncle scoffed at that.

'Nonsense. There's no such thing as bad luck. All those things that happened were just coincidences. They would have happened even if you hadn't touched anyone. When your dad was arrested for bumping into that police car, he obviously wasn't concentrating on his driving.'

Lucky didn't like to hear that. And he didn't believe it. For people kept having bad luck after he touched them. For years and years it never stopped.

Except to his uncle, it seemed. He had a very happy life. He was married to a wonderful woman, had two children who were very successful when they grew up. One became a doctor, the other a lawyer. The uncle lived to a ripe old age, without any bad luck at all, even though he had ruffled Lucky's hair just to show him how foolish he was to believe that he was the cause of so much bad luck.

But then, the day before he was to celebrate his one hundredth birthday, he died of a heart attack. He'd so looked forward to the party with all his family there, but bad luck had befallen him at last. He should never have ruffled Lucky's hair, should he?

Lucky lived to an old age too. He actually did celebrate his one hundredth birthday. He'd had no bad luck in life at all. He'd become famous as a novelist, earning lots of money. One has to be lucky for that to happen. It must have been because he was immune to himself.

So he did have a party.

Unfortunately, no one came to it.

THE KING'S CROWN

There was once a king who couldn't decide which crown to wear. He had so many different ones he was spoilt for choice. He would stand in front of the mirror all day, trying on one after the other to see which he liked most. There was a spiky one; a spiky one with knobs on the spikes; a bulbous one with a red velvet top; umpteen bejewelled ones – one with rubies, one with diamonds, one with sapphires, one with emeralds and several with a mixture of all kinds; a silver one which he deemed more suitable for a queen … And plenty more besides. He couldn't make up his mind. But until he did, he refused to go outside for fear he'd look like an ordinary, run-of-the mill citizen. What king would ever want to do that?

One day he had an idea. He decided to summon all the wise men and women in the land to come to the palace to advise him. They didn't hesitate. They all hoped to get into the king's good books by helping him. If he accepted the advice of any one of them, that person might be offered a permanent position in the palace.

So they turned up on horseback, in wagons and even on foot despite the distance they had to travel. But on the day specified for the meeting, most of them were present. The king welcomed them and took them into a large hall, where the crowns were laid out on a huge table. The wise men and women took their places round the table, and the king told them to inspect the crowns carefully before reaching a decision. He realised that disagreement was inevitable, but he wanted reasons for their choices. Without reasons, their chosen crowns would be no more than mere whims.

'Might we pick the crowns up and feel them, Your Majesty?' asked one respectfully through a thick walrus moustache.

'You may,' allowed the king. 'But don't try to slip one in your pocket. I'm watching closely.'

There were mutterings of 'Indeed not' and 'Well, I won't' from all around the table. One or two of the wise men and women refused to pick up any for fear they might be suspected of doing such a wicked thing. They leaned over the table and studied the crowns closely without touching them. One of the wise women, however, couldn't resist putting the silver crown on her head to see if it fitted, but this brought gasps of outrage from the others and a scowl from the king, so she took it off again smartly.

'This one is extremely heavy,' observed a wise man with shaggy eyebrows. Surprisingly, he was referring to one of the smaller crowns. It was made of solid iron with jewels all around it. 'Wearing this all the time would give me a headache. And we wouldn't want to give our king a headache.' He smiled at the king when he said that. 'So no, not this one.' He almost threw the crown back on the table in disgust.

The wise men and women started discussing the crowns in earnest now. Disagreements occurred, as the king had expected, but reasons for their choices were given, so things seemed to be proceeding sensibly.

Then a younger wise man spoke up. 'You should wear a woolly bob cap instead of a crown. That's not heavy, would be warm in winter –'

'What's a woolly bob cap?' the king wanted to know. He was only used to wearing crowns.

'A cap knitted in wool,' explained the other. 'Sometimes it has a bob on top, rather like those knobs on top of the spiky crowns – but bobs likewise made of wool. I think one would suit Your Majesty.'

'Poppycock!' snapped a wise man with grey hair. 'A woolly bob cap on Your Majesty's head would not look dignified.' He shook his head as if the whole idea was ridiculous.

'I'm not so sure about that,' said one of the wise women, who considered herself an expert on fashion. 'Woolly bob caps come in all styles and colours. One could be specially designed for Your Majesty, with the royal coat of arms at the front.'

The king liked the idea of that. Any display of the royal coat of arms was something he always approved of.

'I could design the bob cap myself,' the wise woman added, eager to please the king.

'I strongly advise Your Majesty not to consider bob caps,' persisted the grey-haired wise man.

'I am curious to see what they're like,' said the king. 'Yes, design one for me and I'll decide if it's suitable when it's on my head.'

So the meeting broke up, with disbelieving looks on the faces of those who opposed the idea – who thought it quite mad, in fact.

The following day, the wise woman who had promised to design a bob cap presented it to the king. She had spent all night knitting it. And being very wise *and* a good knitter she had made a super job of it. As befitted a royal personage, it was made of golden wool, with the royal coat of arms in blue and red, depicting a royal ostrich, as it should.

The king couldn't have been more delighted. He decided at once that he would wear the bob cap instead of a crown. He walked up and down the hall, showing it off on his head to all the wise men and women. A few of them applauded to confirm to the king how much they approved his decision. More than a few didn't.

'You should go skiing in that bob cap,' said the younger wise man who had suggested the bob cap in the first place. 'Lots of people who wear bob caps go skiing.'

'Skiing? What – on skis?' queried the king. He knew what skiing was, but of course he'd never thought of doing it himself.

'Yes. There's a splendid resort for skiing in the mountains to the north. It's where I come from.'

'I strongly advise Your Majesty not to go skiing,' objected the grey-haired wise man. 'It wouldn't look dignified.' He was repeating himself now. The king hated people to repeat themselves, so he paid no attention. In fact, he made up his mind there and then that he would go skiing.

And he did. Preparations were made, and a week later he went off with his bob cap to Brockeleg, a small village at the foot of a snowy mountain. Being a wise man himself, he had a few lessons first and then decided to show how good he was by skiing down the mountainside. Wearing his bob cap, of course.

Unfortunately, even after his lessons, he wasn't that good, and he came a cropper. He broke his left leg. He was in great pain all the way back to the palace. Now, of course, he wished he'd never heard of bob caps, and blamed the younger wise man completely. He ordered him to be arrested and his head to be chopped off. So he was back where he started, wondering which crown to wear.

He hobbled on crutches to the huge table where all the crowns were still laid out.

'Oh, any will do,' he muttered, and picked up the nearest one. It was one with spikes all the way round. He lifted it to his head, meaning to put it on top, but jabbed his face with one of the spikes. He hated the sight of blood, and when some started to seep out of his cheek, he hurled the crown away. He would never wear a crown or anything else on his head again.

Next day, he declared as much to the citizens from the palace balcony, thinking they would like to know. But the response was not what he'd expected. They didn't want a king without a crown – or a bob cap, for that matter. If he wasn't prepared to wear one, they didn't want him for their king.

So they chased him out of the country, even though he was on crutches, and made someone else king instead.

THE TEACHER WHO LIKED TO SCOLD

Miss Peevish swung round and glared at her pupils.

'Silence, Clara. You too, Barbara. And you, Robert. And you, Graham. And you, Deborah. I heard you all whispering. You should be concentrating on what I'm writing on the blackboard, not chattering as if you didn't care tuppence about learning anything. That goes for you too, Terry Mossop. You're as bad as anyone. And if you weren't whispering then, it's only because you'd run out of things to say....'

The children listened, as they were bound to. They couldn't avoid it. Every day she found something to complain about and go on and on about it. Now she was picking on Susan Ratcliffe, who hardly ever said anything, being so shy.

'I just hope you aren't getting into bad habits, Susan, being in a class with these other children. They're a bad influence, and you should know better than to listen to them. Put your hands over your ears when they're talking, and take them away when I'm talking. That, I assure you, is the best policy....'

Clara leaned forward, put her elbows on the desk and rested her chin on her hands. She sighed, and looked across to Simon, who couldn't help grinning at how Miss Peevish was ranting on. Every day it was the same. For one reason or another, their teacher would find something to give the children a ticking-off which went on for half the lesson. Oh, how Clara wished she'd give it a rest. She was just about to wish something nasty about Miss Peevish when Arnold accidentally knocked an exercise book off his desk. It banged on the floor. Miss Peevish whipped round and seemed to know immediately who the culprit was.

'You clumsy oaf!' she screamed. 'Just when I'm teaching you all something important, you go and make a racket like that. Not to mention how dirty your book will be now. Nor how creased the pages will be.' She raised a hand and extended her forefinger. She had a way of pointing at all the children even though it never moved away from Arnold. 'I'm warning you all now, I won't take any more of this bad behaviour. I want silence. I demand silence. I'm the teacher and I say what's what. Understand? Pick it up, boy. Don't sit there like a dummy. The longer the book's on the floor, the dirtier it gets. Any scientist will tell you that.'

At last she turned back to the blackboard and carried on writing numbers down with her chalk.

Arnold sulkily retrieved the book, And he started thinking of something nasty to happen to Miss Peevish. As did a number of the other children. As did most of them, in fact.

The school day ended eventually. But the children didn't rush home. Called together by Clara, she proposed that they do something about their awful teacher. They had to get rid of her, so a nicer teacher could take her place. She asked for suggestions. No one, however, could come up with anything that would work.

'I just wish she'd retire,' said Sheila.

'I wish get a sore throat so she couldn't talk,' grinned Simon.

'I wish she'd have an accident and have to spend a year in hospital,' said Terry Mossop.

Other children were of the same or similar mind. It was what gave Clara the idea.

'We're all wishing for things to stop her scolding us, so that's what we'll do. It might work.'

'What might work?' Simon asked.

'Wishing. We'll all wish her to stop scolding us. We'll do it together, at the same time. We'll do it tomorrow in class, as soon as she starts picking on one of us. If we wish hard enough, it might stop her. She might feel the force of what we feel.'

One or two doubted it would work, but the others were all for it. They had nothing to lose, so why not?

The following morning, before Miss Peevish appeared, Clara told the others that she'd count to three at the right time, and after she said 'three', they should all start wishing that Miss Peevish would stop scolding them.

'Wish as hard as you can,' she insisted, 'and keep wishing till she stops.'

Miss Peevish entered the classroom bang on time. She was never late, and woe betide any child who turned later than she did. That didn't happen today, and Miss Peevish began the lesson.

Till Barbara had a coughing fit.

'Will you stop that racket!' yelled Miss Peevish. 'If it's not someone dropping books on the floor, interrupting my lesson, it's someone coughing herself silly. I can't have these constant attempts to interfere with the job I'm trying to do – for your sakes, I might add. I don't do this for my own sake, you know. I'm doing it for you, so you'll ...'

That's quite enough, thought Clara. It was time to do what they'd planned. She turned round to the other children.

'One ... two ... three!'

The others responded at once. They started wishing ... then wished harder and harder ... and then wished with ever greater intensity. Deborah's eye almost popped out of their sockets. Even the shy Susan was trying her best. And Terry Mossop … he was lifting himself off his seat so fervently was he wishing.

At first nothing seemed to happen for all their efforts. Miss Peevish went on scolding them all as if her life depended on doing it.

Then something did happen. As the words came out of her mouth with increasing venom, so too did a worm.

Just one to begin with. A slimy worm which showed its head first and then its long body before it fell to the ground. Miss Peevish was so engrossed in scolding the children that it seemed she hadn't noticed. But then two more worms emerged from her mouth. Yes, two this time. Two heads and two bodies, before they too fell to the ground. Miss Peevish had certainly noticed those. She fell silent in shock. But that didn't stop three more worms making an appearance. At which point Miss Peevish screamed in horror and ran from the classroom.

'We did it,' boasted Terry Mossop. 'We've got rid of the horrible woman.'

'She might come back yet,' cautioned Clara. 'But it serves her right if those worms keep coming out of her mouth. She's got what she deserved for being so awful.'

There were similar remarks made by other children. 'Horrid' and 'mean' and 'cruel' and 'vicious' were just some of the words used to describe their teacher.

But then something they hadn't expected occurred.

To Clara first.

A worm's head appeared between her lips, followed by its body, before it fell to the ground.

Then it happened to Terry Mossop. Only one worm at first.

Then to Barbara and to Simon.

Then to the others.

And after one worm, it was two worms – which the children kept spitting out in disgust.

You see, whether it's a teacher being nasty to children or children being nasty to their teacher – or anyone else, for that matter – worms will make an appearance eventually. Best not to be nasty or cruel or vicious or horrid at all.

And never to scold children.

At least, that's what they say.

THE SHINY KNIGHT

Hiram Goodleaf was a farmer. A hard-working one, but one who was weary of mowing fields and milking cows. He didn't want to spend the rest of his life doing things like that. He wanted to do something more glamorous – namely, to be a knight in shining armour who fought battles with an enemy. Being a farmer, he had a horse to ride, but he didn't have a suit of armour. And in those days the most formidable knights all wore suits of armour. His mother suggested he go to the market. You can buy things dirt cheap there, she told him. So Hiram went off to the market and started browsing round the stalls.

Sure enough, he found a stall specialising in items of war, including armour. He was quite taken by one suit in particular. It was his size and shone magnificently.

'It's a very special suit of armour, this one,' declared the shifty-eyed seller. 'I would have bought it for myself but it's a bit too small for me.' He patted his tummy. 'Not as fit as I used to be.'

Hiram believed every word he said, so they struck a deal and he went home with his new suit of armour and a sword he'd also bought.

When he put the armour on, his mother was wonderstruck at how glorious he looked.

'You should give yourself a proper knight's name now you're wearing that,' she said.

Hiram pondered. 'I shall call myself the Shiny Knight of Shorley, seeing as Shorley is where we live.'

When he climbed on his horse, he looked even more impressive. Some of his neighbours gasped in admiration as he trotted off to wage war wherever he could find one.

So brightly did his armour shine as the sun beat down that he could have been seen from miles away. He rather resembled a lighthouse without a sea. All that surrounded him were fields and woods and farmhouses like the one he'd left behind.

Before long, though, the weather changed. Clouds gathered – dark, angry clouds, which foretold a spell of rain. More than that, actually. A torrent of rain fell for all of two hours. The Shiny Knight of Shorley tried to take cover under some trees for a while, but the rain poured through the leaves and bounced off his helmet. That was one good thing. But it got under his armour and soaked him through and through.

Eventually the rain stopped and the Shiny Knight rode on. But now something happened to his suit of armour. He hardly noticed at first, till it started creaking. He looked at the breastplate carefully. It seemed to be rusting. It was losing its shiny lustre and turning a copper-brown colour. A rust colour, in other words.

It *was* rusting.

Not to worry, he thought. One suit of armour was much like another. But he couldn't keep a name like the Shiny Knight of Shorley under the circumstances. He decided to call himself the Rusty Knight of Rutland instead. Rutland was the county he came from.

On he rode, seeking the battlefield that so far had eluded him. It wasn't pleasant riding in a shirt and trousers that were wringing wet. And another downpour didn't help. What's more, he started feeling uncomfortable in his suit of armour. It seemed tighter than it had – not just round the torso but also round the legs and arms. He almost laughed at the thought of such a thing, but it seemed to be shrinking. Armour didn't shrink, surely.

Yet when he started finding it difficult to breathe because his chest couldn't expand, he had to face the horrible truth: it *was* shrinking – and shrinking fast.

He jumped from his horse and started pulling the armour off. If it became too tight, he might never be able to get it off. He might never be able to breathe in it.

He was just in time, it seemed. The breastplate came off, the greaves protecting the legs came off, the arm guards came off, but how difficult it was to get his shoes off. They had become so tight that he had to pull and pull before he managed to do it.

'What a useless piece of junk,' he muttered. He was now standing there in his wet underclothes – hardly the picture of a great warrior. It had stopped raining again, but his clothes were still wet through. He'd be better without them on, he decided. He could dry his skin in the sun, which he couldn't do if he kept his clothes on.

So he tore his clothes off and stood there in the nude.

Not to worry, he thought again. He still had his sword. He picked it up, remounted his horse, flourished the sword in a warlike way and wondered what to call himself now. He was no longer the Rusty Knight of Rutland. He was … what? The Naked Knight of … of … Notastitchon.

He kicked the sides of the horse with his heels and off they went. The Naked Knight of Notastitchon and his tireless steed.

Actually, his horse was getting tired, but it didn't matter. For within a mile or two, he saw in the distance a mass of men – soldiers, he realised. They'd reached the battlefield. He kicked his horse with his heels again to urge it to canter. As he approached the soldiers – some of them on foot, some on horseback – they turned to gawk at him. Well, they would. The Naked Knight of Notastitchon was an extraordinary sight. He was coming straight towards them – straight *at* them, it seemed. Was he on their side, or on the enemy's side? Those directly in the horse's path stepped aside to let it through. The Naked Knight waved his sword in the air, eager to get to grips with the enemy, whom he could see now about a hundred yards away. He didn't bring his horse to a halt. He heeled it again, urging it to a gallop.

Up ahead, the enemy couldn't believe their eyes. Was this a madman heading their way? He wasn't wearing any clothes. He had no protection … no suit of armour … nothing. Was he immune to any of their weapons … to their arrows and their swords? What fiend was this?

'Well, I'm not sticking round to find out,' muttered one of the enemy, who immediately turned and ran for his life. He was quickly followed by others. They'd never fought against a naked man before, and the way he flourished his sword about showed he meant business with it. Soon hundreds of them were fleeing. And then the rest of them did the same.

The Naked Knight of Notastitchon was the hero of the hour. The enemy had been vanquished without a blow having been struck. The other soldiers gathered round him, cheering and crying, 'Well done, mate.'

The Naked Knight was pleased at being acclaimed like that, but it was when the King arrived that he realised what he'd achieved.

'You are our hero on this day,' the King said in a solemn tone, 'and shall be justly rewarded. You shall be knighted at once. Jump off your horse so I can perform the ceremony.'

Well, it was one thing to be the Naked Knight of Notastitchon, but quite another to be *Sir* Naked Knight of Notastitchon. So, beaming with pride, the Naked Knight leapt off his horse, landing on his two bare feet.

Right on some nettles. How he jumped and danced about as his feet landed on one clump of nettles after another. He was squealing with pain as the soldiers around him were laughing their heads off.

The Naked Knight could hardly keep still as he knelt down – placing his knees on another clump of nettles – so the King could touch his shoulders with his sword.

'Arise sir knight,' said the King when he'd finished. 'Sir Dancing Knight of Nettles – this is the name I give you in memory of this great day.'

Sir Dancing Knight of Nettles didn't mind the new name. To be honoured by the King with a knighthood was beyond his wildest dreams. He set out for home in a borrowed set of clothes. After all, he was no longer the Naked Knight and needed something to wear.

But he still had no shoes on. The nettles had made his feet very painful and itchy. He couldn't stop scratching them all the way back to his farm. He was given a hero's welcome again when the villagers learned of his heroics. But for a long long time, he couldn't wash his feet. Using soap and water on them made them smart and sting. So he left them as they were, getting more and more muck and dirt on them every day.

And so he soon became known as the Smelly Farmer of Bare Feet.

And that's how he's known to this day ... though he does insist on *Sir* Smelly Farmer of Bare Feet.

THE DOLL AND THE TOY SOLDIER

Uncle Willy was upset. He had no children of his own, and there was nothing he liked more than to give his niece and nephew a present each at Christmas. To see their happy faces when they saw what he'd brought them made him just as happy as they were. This year, however, he had to go abroad on business and wouldn't be with them on Christmas Day. All he could do was buy their presents and have the shop send them before the big day arrived. He knew what they wanted – they'd been telling him for weeks. Margaret wanted a doll, Gordon a toy soldier. And because he didn't want to show favouritism, he made sure that neither one was bigger than the other, give or take a fraction of an inch. The doll he chose wore a pink dress, while the toy soldier had a blue tunic and was carrying a rifle over his shoulder. He gave the shop assistant the delivery address, then went off on his business trip to goodness knows where.

Margaret and Gordon couldn't have cared less where he'd gone as long as he'd bought them something for Christmas. When they saw the presents at the foot of the Christmas tree, they eagerly tore off the colourful wrapping paper and ripped off the lids from the boxes.

But how their faces fell! Margaret looked with dismay at the toy soldier. She hadn't wanted one of those. Gordon was crestfallen. What was a six-year-old boy like him to do with a doll in a pink dress? When Margaret saw what Gordon had, she was near to tears. It was just like him to get the best presents, she thought. And when Gordon saw how lucky she had been to get a toy soldier, he was distraught. It wasn't just the toy soldier. She had a toy rifle as well. His doll hadn't got one. Dolls never had rifles.

Their parents had been enjoying the sight of their children drooling over their presents. But when they saw how they reacted to Uncle Willy's, they realised something was wrong. They checked the names and addresses on the discarded wrapping paper, and of course they saw that each of the presents had been addressed to the wrong child. The stupid assistant must have mixed them up.

'It's just a mistake,' their mother explained. 'Just swap them, so you, Margaret, can have the doll and you, Gordon, can have the toy soldier.'

A very reasonable suggestion, you might think.

But not to Margaret or Gordon.

'It's mine!' said Margaret, retreating with the toy soldier in case her mother tried to take it from her.

And 'This is mine!' insisted Gordon, hugging the doll. He had no intention of being left with no presents while Margaret had two.

'Oh, come now,' put in their father. 'Surely you can see what's happened. You should have received each other's present. Uncle Willy wouldn't have bought you a doll, Gordon, or you a soldier, Margaret. He obviously meant you to have the other ones. Just swap them; then you'll both have what you wanted.'

A very reasonable confirmation of what their mother had said.

But not to Margaret or Gordon.

'It's mine,' sulked Margaret from the far corner of the room. The more she repeated those words, the more she liked the present she had, and the more determined she was to keep it. Uncle Willy had bought it for her.

Likewise, Gordon had no intention of giving up the doll. It was a present from Uncle Willy. He didn't like the doll – in fact, he hated it. But it was his and no one else's.

He also hated Margaret for having a toy soldier. Naturally, Margaret felt the same about him for having the doll. They glowered at each other, clutching their presents all the more firmly.

Their parents decided to let them have their way for the time being. They were sure to change their minds. Especially Gordon. He wouldn't want to be playing with a doll for very long. And Margaret was bound to get more and more jealous when she saw him with it.

They had other presents too – quite a few from their parents. But those were ignored. The doll and the toy soldier were the only ones they seemed to care about. Margaret pretended to be shooting with the rifle. Gordon started to make a fuss about arranging the doll's clothes, pulling the pink dress down. Margaret had the soldier marching off as if to war. Gordon had the doll saying 'Daddy' to him.

It couldn't go on, of course. Their parents were right about that. Soon the two children were shouting at each other. Their parents tried to calm them down, but it only got worse. Margaret used the toy soldier to hit Gordon, who was quick to give her a whack with the doll. Then they started bashing the doll and the toy soldier together, as if they wanted to damage the one the other had. It seemed they didn't care that the ones they were using might also be damaged. After all, what did Margaret really care about a toy soldier? And Gordon didn't care tuppence about a doll in a pink dress.

Sure enough, before their parents could intervene, both the doll and the toy soldier were battered to pieces. Arms and legs and heads had come off. The only thing left in Margaret's hand was one of the toy soldier's legs. Likewise, in Gordon's hand – one of the doll's legs.

'Now look what you've done,' their mother scolded them. 'Your Uncle Willy's presents ruined. He won't be pleased when he sees them like that.'

The two children's heads drooped. They realised now that they'd gone too far.

'You shouldn't be so silly,' their father said. 'There was no need for you to carry on like that over a couple of presents.' He gave a deep sigh. 'Well … I'll see if I can put them together again.'

And so he did. It took him till the following day, but he managed to do it in his own way. Deliberately so. He knew exactly what he was doing. He put one of the soldier's arms onto the doll. He fixed one of the doll's legs to the soldier. He attached the soldier's head to the doll's body and gave the doll his rifle. He dressed the soldier in the pink dress.

Then he gave the doll to Margaret and the soldier to Gordon.

That is to say, he gave a mixture of both to each of them

'That should keep you satisfied for a while,' he said, with a smile to their mother. 'You've both got bits of them now.'

The bemused children looked with dismay at the curious objects in their hands. They weren't what Uncle Willy had bought them.

So no, they weren't satisfied at all.

But then, children seldom are.

THE BOY WHO WANTED TO BE ...

First of all he wanted to be a footballer. A star player for his favourite team. And for England, of course. He'd dreamt of it since he was old enough to kick a ball. But that was all he could do – kick it. When he tried to control the ball – the most important skill a footballer could possess – he kept stumbling over it. Whenever he shot at goal, he missed by yards. His dad tried to help him, telling him not to toe-poke the ball but to hit it with his instep. So he did it that way, but he still missed the goal by yards. When he tried to head the ball, it usually hit him in the face. And, at school, whenever he tried to tackle anyone, he would miss the ball and catch the other player on the ankle, causing an injury which often got him sent off.

Eventually he had to admit that football wasn't the game for him. So he tried his hand at cricket. He could see himself hitting sixes all around the ground, and taking ten wickets in one innings with his bowling. But when he swung the bat, he missed the ball and found the stumps behind him shattered – out for a duck usually. When he took the ball to bowl his off-spin, it was then that sixes were hit, the batsmen finding no difficulty in swatting his deliveries all over the place.

Instead of cricket, he took up long-distance running, and went out jogging with his dad. There was nothing his dad would have liked more than to see his son become good at something, and if he could help him he would. But after they'd run a hundred yards, his son was usually gasping for breath; and he hadn't enjoyed even the hundred yards he'd managed.

So he turned against sport altogether. He took up music. His mother played the piano, and he pestered her to teach him. She did, willingly. She was just as eager to help her son as his dad was. But he could never master the scales she gave him to practise. His fingers could never press on one note at a time. It was always two together – which caused his mother to clap her hands over her ears in despair at the clunking. Even simple tunes sounded like different ones, but different ones that weren't played very well. He persuaded her to buy him a recorder. He'd do better with that, he promised.

But promises aren't always kept, and he could never get his fingers over the right holes to play the tune he intended. So the recorder ended up in the bin. His mother retrieved it when she found out what he'd done with it, but he never touched it again.

Being such a determined young boy, he wasn't prepared to give up on music straight away, so he thought of being a drummer. Neither his mother nor his father was too keen on that, as drums do make a lot of noise. But ever keen to encourage their son, they bought him a set. He could bang about on it in the basement; he wouldn't disturb anyone there. He hardly had time to do so. He banged the drum so hard that the drumstick broke. He had to get another, much thicker one. But as soon as he started pounding the drum with that, he smashed the drum. That too ended up in the bin, but neither his mother nor his father retrieved it.

Music disappeared from his life, and painting took its place. And what a mess he made of himself when it did. He got more paint on his clothes and his person than he did on the canvas. His mother had to wash the clothes, so she wasn't best pleased at how slapdash he was. And, although she wouldn't admit it, his paintings didn't impress her. Was that really a tree – and that a hippopotamus? And that giraffe had a neck like a snake's and a body like a rabbit's.

The easel ended up in the bin, along with some of his clothes which were just too covered in paint to make clean again.

So then he decided to be very clever, and started working hard at school. He'd never been good at sums, and much as he tried, he didn't become any better. He kept missing commas out in his English lessons, despite constant complaints from his teacher. Commas seemed such tiddly things, he thought it was hardly worth the bother of remembering where to put them. History he couldn't see the point of either. One date was much like another to him. Did it really matter if a battle was fought in 1066 and not 1232 or 1463?

But then Geography started to interest him more than anything else.

It was all those maps. Maps of other countries. Maps of unexplored places, where untold mysteries awaited the brave explorer who ventured into the dark unknown.

He would be an explorer, he decided. The best there had ever been. He wasn't old enough to set off on an expedition yet, so he decided to practise by exploring the streets near where he lived. Some of them he already knew, of course, so he wasn't really exploring them. It was only when he turned down streets he hadn't been in before that he felt he really was an explorer. Left into Algernon Street, then right into Laira Street. Then right into Warley Street and left into Goode Street. Round the corner into

Chandler Avenue and straight on till he reached Daresbury Road, when he turned right till he came to Holland Street and turned right again. Then … he couldn't think how to get back home. He was lost. His parents started worrying after three hours and contacted the police. A search was started and eventually he was found. He'd got fed up with trying to find his way home, so he changed his mind about being an explorer. All those changes of direction were confusing. Much better if there was only one direction to think about.

So he decided to become a mountaineer. There was only one direction that mattered when climbing mountains, and that was up. So he started practising. That meant climbing the stairs at home again and again. He did that after school – all evening. He would tramp up the stairs, then come down again, then climb up again, then come down again. He did it a hundred times the first evening and two hundred times the next. His legs got stronger with every step he took, whether up or down. His parents were both pleased and proud. They thought their son was at last going to become good at something.

Then he overdid it. He tried to climb the stairs five hundred times in an evening. But his legs weren't strong enough for that. By the time he'd managed 456 times, his legs were buckling, and on the 457th time as he reached the top of the stairs, they couldn't support him any more. He fell all the way downstairs and broke his ankle.

He spent the next few weeks in bed, unable to walk. He slept a lot. After all his efforts to be a footballer or a cricketer or a long-distance runner or a painter or a pianist or an explorer or a mountaineer, he was exhausted. All he wanted to do was sleep.

And snore. His parents had never heard him snore before. But now they couldn't avoid it. His snoring was surprisingly loud for a little boy. It was loud for anyone, never mind a little boy. He was a very good snorer. They did what they could to stop him. After all, they didn't want to keep hearing that all night. It stopped them from sleeping. So they would wake him up, hoping that when he dozed off again he wouldn't start snoring again. But he always did. They gave him sleeping pills to see if that would stop him. But it never did. He was such a good snorer.

And despite his parents' continued efforts to stop him, he remained a good snorer for the rest of his life.

They should have been pleased, but I don't think they were.

THE WELL

In a village too far away for anyone to know where it was, the people who lived there were expecting something to happen. Something important. Something that would change their lives for evermore. They didn't know what it was, but they would have been foolish not to take into account all the rumours and prophecies. Virtually everyone had a guess at what it might be, and different people had different views on how to react to whatever it was. Some were frightened, assuming the worst. Some said they'd take it in their stride, however bad it was.

'There's no point in despairing,' remarked an elderly man with a walking stick. 'I've suffered from evil times before. I'm not going to abandon all hope for a better life if misfortune befalls us again.'

'I agree to a point,' said the baker's wife. 'I just hope it doesn't result in a shortage of flour for our bread. My husband and I are already struggling to make ends meet. If it gets any worse, we'll end up as beggars on the street.'

Nobody believed that. The baker's wife was always complaining about one thing or another. She and her husband had plenty of money; they just didn't like to admit it in case burglars broke into their house.

'Well, let's not hope for too much,' counselled a tubby man, who preferred to be called wise rather than tubby. 'We're bound to be disappointed if we do. I'd rather keep an open mind on what to expect, and be disappointed only if nothing at all happens.'

'You can't mean that,' objected the bald-headed grocer. 'What if something truly terrible happens? Wouldn't you be disappointed then, when something so much better could have happened instead?'

The tubby man pondered. He didn't like to lose any argument, and often chose to fall silent when he looked like doing so.

'Oh, that reminds me,' he said, and hurried away.

A little girl with a very glum face was standing by the well in the village square.

'I hope it's not because I'm going to fall down the well,' she said. She had often peered down it and got dizzy thinking how far down it went.

'Don't be silly,' her mother said, with a shake of her head at how silly her little girl could be. 'Stay away from the well and you'll never fall down it, so it wouldn't happen, would it?'

The baker's wife agreed. 'Yes, don't be stupid. I'm glad I've not got a little girl as stupid as you are. Just stay away from the well, as you're mother says. Nobody will fall down the well if they go nowhere near it.'

'I think it'll be a plague of wasps that swarm about stinging everyone,' said a little boy who was just as silly as the little girl. He liked the idea of wasps no more than she did of the well. Wasps can sting.

Just then, before he could make his feelings known, the owner of small tavern cried out.

'There's someone coming on a donkey.'

Everyone looked in the direction indicated. Yes, there was a man on a donkey. This could be it. Something was bound to happen now. There was nothing unusual about seeing anyone on a donkey in these parts, but this was different. The villagers had been waiting so long for something to happen that they wouldn't tolerate it, they thought, if the man let them down.

Slowly the donkey ambled towards them. Oh, why couldn't donkeys be as fast as horses? They hardly seemed to be moving most of the time. The nearer the man on its back came, the more his features stood out. He was gaunt with a heavily lined face. He was dressed in long dirty clothes, and was either poor or, by the looks of him, a hard worker, or both. As he reached them, he raised his hand and greeted them, but didn't stop. He went on through the village and didn't even turn his head to look back as he disappeared round a bend in the road.

'You should have said something,' said the baker's wife to the bald-headed grocer.

'Me? Why me?'

'You're a man. You can't expect a woman to accost a man who's just passing through. What would people think? We may never know now what's going to happen.'

'Well, if we never know, it must mean it won't happen.'

'But it might. We'll be on tenterhooks for evermore. That little girl will keep thinking she's going to fall down the well. She'll drive us all crazy.'

The grocer could see the truth of what she'd said. 'Well, it's too late now. Maybe someone else is coming along behind him. That's when the trouble could start – if there's going to be any.'

'Or the wasps may come,' suggested the little boy, who had been eavesdropping on their conversation.

The grocer had no time for little boys who thought they knew more than he did.

'Or the bees or the locusts,' he snorted. 'Or the lions or the buffalo or the elephants …' He kept on muttering like that as he went back into his shop.

'Pay no attention to him,' the woman said. 'It may well be wasps. It wouldn't surprise me at all. More likely that than anyone falling down the well.'

Having said which, she sneered at the little girl, who was still gazing glumly at it. She wasn't convinced yet that she wouldn't fall down it. Her mother had told her to stay away from it, but she had always liked peering into the depths, which seemed interesting and mysterious. For the moment, though, she kept her distance from it. Once something else happened, she would go and look down it again.

Unless it had happened already, of course. And it wasn't long before rumours to that effect began to spread. Just as that man on the donkey had passed through the village with little more than a wave, so too something might have happened without anyone noticing.

'Maybe the wasps have been and gone,' said the little boy, hopefully.

'Well, whatever it was, it hasn't affected our supply of flour,' admitted the baker's wife. 'It's just a pity people aren't buying as much bread as they used to. It's making things very difficult for me and my husband. We've hardly got two pennies to rub together.'

'The well's still there,' grumbled the little girl. 'If nothing has happened, I might still fall down it.'

'Oh, for goodness' sake!' cried the baker's wife. 'Give it a rest. If I was your mother I'd give you a smack No one's going to fall down that well, so stop thinking it. You're driving us all mad with your constant whingeing –'

At which point the tubby man and the bald-headed grocer picked her up and threw her down the well.

The little girl smiled, and everyone lived happily ever after.

Something had happened at last.

THE GREAT MARVO

The audience had come to see the finest magician in the land. He was there on the stage in a colourful costume of gold and orange, with long straggly hair which made him look a bit loopy. He had already performed several very ordinary magic tricks, but now was the moment everyone had been waiting for. Marvo had asked for a volunteer from the audience to step up onto the stage. He was going to make that person disappear.

'Into the realms of non-existence,' he cried out.

There were gasps of anticipation. They'd heard of this trick but had never seen it done before.

'Just one brave person,' Marvo called out. 'Be not afraid of vanishing in physical form. Your entire person will persist in a greater perfection.'

Heads swivelled this way and that as people tried to catch sight of someone who was answering the call. At first no one was. Maybe it was shyness at being the centre of attention. Or maybe it was fear of what lay in store for anyone rash enough to put himself or herself at Marvo's mercy. For that was how it seemed to them – being put at the mercy of a magician.

Marvo pleaded with them. 'Just one with the courage of a lion.'

That did the trick. A rather nervous, slim young man stood up and started squeezing past the people sitting in the same row.

'There is one,' proclaimed Marvo. 'A round of applause, please. Such a brave soul deserves out respect and admiration.'

The audience responded with a burst of enthusiastic clapping. If someone else wanted to disappear in physical form, they were happy enough to watch it happen. The man stumbled as he mounted the steps to the stage.

'Ha-ha!' laughed Marvo. 'The gentleman can't wait to disappear. I've never seen anyone so eager. You're not heavily in debt, are you, and want to escape before you're arrested?'

This brought a roar of laughter from the audience. The man gave a weak smile.

'No, no, nothing like that,' he managed to reply.

'And your name, sir?' Marvo asked.

'Ivor Turnbull,' said the man.

'Well, Ivor, don't be nervous. You are totally in my power from now on, but you have nothing to fear. All I want you to do is lie in this box. Yes, I know it's like a coffin, but that's only because it's ideal for a person to lie in. You are not going to die!' Marvo emphasised these last words, then laughed again, and looked towards the audience, who responded by laughing themselves. Such an idea that a man could die when he was only helping a magician to perform a trick. It was a trick, wasn't it? The man wasn't really going to disappear. That wasn't possible, was it?

Marvo was helping the man into the coffin – er, the box. It was standing on a table supported by four legs, and nothing was underneath it. The audience could see right through to the back of the stage. No question that the man would fall through a collapsible bottom and slide under the stage. That would be a very obvious trick, and wouldn't impress anyone. No; Marvo was actually going to make the man disappear – to make him vanish into thin air.

Or such was Marvo's claim.

Once the man was lying inside the box, Marvo put the lid on so he couldn't be seen by the audience, and then started whirling it round and round. The table had a revolving top. The legs stayed where they were, but the top went round and round.

Marvo held his arms out wide, closed his eyes and seemed to summon up huge reserves of strength. And, with the audience agog at what was about to ensue, he started muttering an incantation – till he came to a very important word.

The word he had to utter before the trick would work.

'Er … er … Gocklepop.' That didn't seem right. 'Googleplop.' Nor did that. What was it? He'd forgotten.

He kept spinning the box on the table, trying to remember what the word was. 'Glockersplot … Gogglesplit … Gagglesplot …' He had never used the word 'Abracadabra'. Only second-rate magicians used that, and he was a very special magician. He used a word that only he would ever think of using. It set him apart from all the others. 'Gloggletot … Glackersplat …' But it had gone completely from his mind.

The audience was getting restless. When was the trick going to be done? But they could still hear Marvo muttering and see the box spinning.

'Get on with it,' someone in the stalls shouted.

Marvo blushed with embarrassment. 'Gloogletoot … Glaggletag …'

More people were urging him now to get the trick done. They'd paid money to see it and they couldn't wait all night. Marvo realised he couldn't delay any longer. He stopped the spinning box and prepared to lift the lid, hoping for the best.

The best being that Ivor wouldn't be inside it.

But Ivor was. He hadn't disappeared. He was still in the realms of existence. As he climbed out of the box and stepped onto the floor, he swayed here and there, so dizzy was he. But how the audience hooted with derision. Shouts of outrage came from all round the theatre.

'You fake! ... Phoney! ... Give us our money back! ...' Someone even threw an ice-cream tub at Marvo, when it wasn't even empty.

Marvo avoided the tub but he was mortified. Ashamed. His reputation was in tatters. And just because he'd forgotten that word. Without it he was a nobody. He dragged himself off the stage in abject misery, before he suffered physical injury from the other objects being hurled his way. He headed for his dressing room and locked the door behind him. He wished with all his heart that he could disappear. He sat in front of his dressing mirror and gazed sadly at his face. And a sad face gazed back at him.

'Gagglepop,' he muttered. ' Glaggertip … Gligglepoop … Gloggertop!'

Having said which, he disappeared with a 'whoof!'.

He couldn't see anything … Couldn't hear or smell anything … Couldn't feel anything.

The face in the mirror had also disappeared.

He didn't know where he was,

Apart from in the realms of non-existence.

But at least he'd remembered what his magic word was.

Without it he was nobody.

THE MOUSE THAT SLEPT IN A STOCKING

It was Christmas Eve. Snow had fallen on the ground and made it a white Christmas. But also a cold one. And especially cold for a mouse that lived under the floorboards at number 12, Kirkstone Terrace. It was chilly in the summer, because the sun never shone there, but it was freezing in winter because draughts swept in through little gaps in the boards. Mice can't take too much cold as their fur is very thin, so this mouse decided to explore the house to find somewhere warmer.

That was why it ended up in Daisy's room. Daisy was a little girl whose bedroom was always kept warm by her parents. They didn't want her catching a cold or the flu. To be honest, she could be a bit of a grumbler at the best of times. But when she was poorly she never stopped complaining. At the moment, though, she was perfectly healthy and fast asleep in her bed.

Looking round the room, the mouse noticed something rather strange: a stocking was hanging from the foot of the bed. Only one, not two. Very puzzling, that – unless the little girl had only one foot. Either way, that stocking would be warm and a good place to get some sleep. The mouse hadn't been sleeping very well of late because of all the shivering it did. The sock would be ideal. Without more ado, the mouse scampered up onto the bed to where it could jump in the stocking. This it did very quickly, then fell to the bottom of the stocking and even more quickly dozed off.

It was very comfortable there and the mouse slept soundly.

Till something woke it in the early hours of the morning.

An object of some sort was dropped into the stocking, and landed squarely on the mouse's tummy. Fortunately, despite the pain it felt, it was able to squirm out from underneath before other things landed on top of the first thing. It would have been squashed completely if it hadn't acted so speedily.

Try as it might, though, it couldn't climb up over whatever the things were, since they were too closely packed together. It couldn't budge from where it was. It had to stay there for ages, wondering if it would ever escape. It was just as capable as Daisy of grumbling, and it did – but only to itself as no one else was there to hear it.

Eventually it heard a woman's voice.

'Come on, Daisy, Wakey-wakey! It's Christmas morning.'

A few minutes passed while Daisy got used to being awake. Then she realised that it was Christmas and that she must have some presents waiting to be opened.

But they'd be downstairs by the tree. The stocking at the foot of the bed was there in her bedroom, so that was what she inspected first. She crawled over her bed to it and started bringing out one thing after another, her face wreathed in smiles at each one. A small bracelet ... a bow for her hair ... a packet of marshmallows ... a packet of coloured pencils ... a mouse ...

A mouse!

A MOUSE!!

The sight of that gave her such a shock that she gave a small yelp of fright and backed away.

But that was nothing to what her mother did. She had been watching with a broad smile on her face as Daisy showed such pleasure in what she'd found in the stocking.

But when Daisy yelped and moved away from the stocking, she too looked inside and –

Her loud scream brought Daisy's father rushing upstairs to find out what the commotion was all about. He was just in time to see the mouse jump out of the stocking and scamper out of sight under the bed. Daisy's mother, on the other hand, had jumped *on* the bed so the mouse couldn't attack her.

'Kill it!' she begged her husband. 'It was a mouse … a mouse in Daisy's stocking.'

Daisy, meanwhile, had calmed down after her initial shock. Her mum was right. It was a mouse in her Christmas stocking. Santa Claus must have left it for her. It was a present.

'No, don't kill it,' she said. 'Father Christmas left it for me. It's mine.'

'Don't be silly, Daisy,' retorted her mother. 'Father Christmas wouldn't leave a live mouse for you. It must have jumped in when you were asleep.'

'It didn't,' insisted Daisy. 'It's mine. I want it.'

Her father was peering under the bed, trying to catch sight of it; but mice are very good are hiding when they want to be. He couldn't spot it anywhere.

'It's mine,' repeated Daisy, forlornly.

'I'm not having mice running about in this house,' said her mother. 'And if Father Christmas did leave it for you, he ought to be ashamed of himself. Mice are frightening to some children.'

'Not to me,' declared Daisy. 'I like cuddly little animals.'

'Cuddly? A mouse cuddly?' Daisy's mother couldn't believe her ears. She turned to Daisy's father, 'We'll have to get someone in to put poison down.'

'No!' shrieked Daisy. 'You can't poison it. It's my mouse. Father Christmas –'

'Yes, yes, we know. Father Christmas left it for you. But we're still going to poison it.' Saying which, Daisy's mother at last got down from the bed and hurriedly left the room.

'Come on, Daisy,' said her father. 'You'd better come down and see the rest of your presents. You can't stay here alone with a mouse at large.'

But Daisy wouldn't move. She was sulking, and when Daisy sulked, it was hard to get her to do anything. So her father left her. She'd come down soon enough when she thought of all those presents at the foot of the tree.

Not so. As soon as her father had gone, Daisy hopped out of bed and got down on her knees, looking round for the mouse.

'Mousey!' she said in a whisper so as not to scare it. 'Mousey, mousey. It's all right, They've gone. I won't hurt you.' The mouse stayed hidden, wherever it was. Daisy got up and went to the presents taken from the stocking. She got the packet of marshmallows, took one out and dropped to her knees again.

'Mousey, mousey. I've got a nice marshmallow here for you.' She held out the marshmallow in different directions, hoping the mouse would smell the chocolate on the outside. Even mice couldn't resist chocolate, she was sure.

This mouse obviously couldn't, for almost straight away its head popped into view from behind the leg of the bed. Daisy could see its nose sniffing the chocolate. She slowly pushed the marshmallow closer to it. The mouse inhaled deeply – then couldn't resist it any more. It scurried over to the marshmallow and started eating it.

Daisy watched for a while with a smile on her face, then gently picked the mouse up. The mouse didn't mind. It sensed it was in no danger from this little girl, who now got to her feet and climbed on the bed, where she sat with the mouse on her lap still eating what was left of the marshmallow.

Such a tiny thing the mouse was, she thought, stroking it with the tip of her forefinger.

Just then, the door opened slightly and her mother's head popped round it,

'Come on, Daisy,' she began. 'You've got lots of pres–'

She froze as she caught sight of the mouse on her daughter's lap.

But only for a second. Then she yelled.

'A-a-a-a-rgh!' She was torn between rushing to rescue Daisy from the terrible creature and escaping while she could.

The mouse had turned to look at her. It was that woman again – the one who wanted to put poison down to kill it, the one who had said mice are frightening to some children. The mouse objected very strongly to that. It never wanted to frighten anyone.

Except right now. It wanted to frighten that woman. So, leaving what was left of the marshmallow till later, it jumped off the bed and scampered towards her. Daisy's mother yelled again, turned on her heels and bolted as fast as she could down the stairs … clatter clatter clatter – and out of the house, with Daisy's father watching in astonishment.

Down the path went Daisy's mother, across the road and over the fields and the distant hill, never stopping for an instant.

But it wasn't that she was running just anywhere.

She was off to the North Pole to give that Santa Claus a right ticking-off.

How dare he bring her daughter a mouse for Christmas.

THE SWEET SHOP

Horace Creep was a snooty man. He looked down his nose at children as if they weren't worth more than threepence each. He didn't like how noisy they were, and was disgusted at how dirty they were. He tried to avoid them at all costs, and wanted more than anything to have nothing to do with them.

But that was difficult: for Horace owned a sweet shop, the only one for miles around. And that meant children were always coming into the shop, wanting to buy sweets. The trouble was they were never sure what to choose. They would hum and hah, looking first at jelly babies, then at dolly mixtures, then at chocolate buttons and other things besides. Only after twenty minutes or so would they decide. Horace hated having to wait. If two or more came together, they would sometimes squabble over what to get. It drove him mad. He would have liked it much more if grown-ups had come to buy the sweets, but they hardly ever did. It was kids kids kids.

He disliked the word 'kids' intensely. He loathed the word 'children'. And the words 'little girls' and 'little boys' made him want to pull his hair out. Yet here he was every day having to sell them sweets.

What he really wanted to be was a juggler in a circus. Ever since he was a little boy himself he had dreamt of it. He'd practised all his life with small balls. First with two – he could do it with them easily. Then with three –

But he was hopeless with three. No matter how hard he tried, the balls kept either bumping into each other or falling to the ground before he could catch them. He had hoped to be able to juggle ten eventually, so he could become the star of the circus. His name would be the largest on the posters. 'The Remarkable Horace' he would call himself. Only he in the world would be so skilful –

Alas, such thinking soon fizzled out when he couldn't even juggle three.

Then, one day, three children came into the shop together. After the usual delay in deciding what to buy, they chose three different kinds of sweets. Glaring at them because they'd taken so long, Horace slapped the three packets on the counter and demanded his money, which was handed over. The packets were picked up by Tommy, who then tossed the liquorice allsorts to Jennifer and the dolly mixtures to Terry. These two children immediately pulled their faces and tossed them back to Tommy. He'd given them the wrong ones. He grinned, having done it on purpose. But then, to the astonishment of all, including Horace especially, he started juggling the three packets of sweets. They didn't bump into each other and they didn't fall to the ground before he caught them.

'How do you do that?' gasped Horace, goggling at him.

'It's easy,' boasted Tommy. 'You just have to get the timing right. Watch.'

Horace was already watching.

'Teach me,' he said, 'and I'll give you another packet of sweets for free.'

So Tommy did. He spent half an hour teaching Horace how to juggle three packets of sweets. It meant Terry and Jennifer had to wait a lot longer to get the sweets they'd chosen, but they did have a laugh or two when Horace kept dropping the packets. It took him ages to get the hang of it, but eventually he did. At last he could juggle three at a time.

He was so pleased with himself. And from then on, too, he was delighted whenever children entered his shop to buy sweets. It gave him the chance to show off his newly acquired skills. Even if they wanted only one packet, he always insisted on giving them two extra for free and treating them to a piece of juggling.

Round and round the packets would go in a blurry circle as Horace tossed them from one hand to the other. The children gaped in wonder at how clever he was.

At least, they did for a few times. But when Horace kept doing it day after day, they realised they'd seen it all before. It was the same thing every time. And children do get bored watching the same thing over and over again.

Of course, they weren't about to stop going in the shop, not when they liked sweets so much. So they discussed the matter among themselves. It was Tommy who suggested what to do.

The next time he and his friends went in the shop, they didn't ask for one packet of sweets ... or for two packets ... or even for three. They asked for four: one of dolly mixtures, one of gobstoppers, one of liquorice allsorts and one of smarties. Horace's face lit up. This was his chance to juggle four packets – to show these children he was even better at juggling than they'd thought.

He picked up the packets, tossed one in the air, then another, while at the same time passing one from one hand to the other, and then –

But before he could catch the first one he'd tossed up it fell to the ground, followed by the second one. He picked them up and tried again ... this time to stifled chuckling from the children. He hardly noticed that. He was concentrating on his juggling. Up in the air the first packet went, up in the air the second packet went … Down to the ground the first packet fell, down to the ground the second packet fell.

The children burst out laughing. Horace couldn't ignore them now. His face turned red with embarrassment. Once again he picked up the packets, and once again he tossed the first one up – but that felt to the ground before he could toss the second one up. All his timing had gone.

And so had the children. They had hurried out of the shop, laughing fit to burst.

Horace glared after them.

Kids!

How he hated that word again.

OVER THE HILL

Young Benjy gazed out from the gate towards the distant hill. He had never been to that hill and he didn't know what lay beyond it. So naturally he was curious. His grandfather was doing some weeding in the garden, so he called out to him.

'Grandad – are there any dragons over that hill?'

His grandfather looked up. 'I've never seen any, but there might be. You mean the sort that can shoot flames out of their mouths?'

'Yes,' said Benjy.

'Not sure I would like to see one if it can do that. I might get burnt.'

Benjy reflected on that. He wouldn't have liked to get burnt either. Still, he would like to see one.

'Are there are any buck-toothed ogres ten feet tall over the hill?' he asked.

'Ah, now there you have me. I'm not sure. They're very shy, ogres. There could be, but I doubt anyone knows for certain. They're very frightening to look at, from what I hear, but they're probably not as bad as they're made out to be.'

'Are there any crocodiles without any teeth over the hill?' Benjy asked next.

'Again, I haven't seen any. But there are rivers, and I wouldn't be surprised if there are some gliding about just waiting to snap their jaws on anyone having a swim.'

'I don't suppose it would hurt very much if they haven't got any teeth,' Benjy pointed out.

'No, but I wouldn't like their jaws clamping down on me, even if they don't have any teeth,' said his grandfather.

'Are there any ostriches jumping about like kangaroos over the hill?' Benjy enquired.

His grandfather gave a puzzled frown. 'I've never heard of anything like that,' he said. 'I tell you what. Why don't we have we have a walk up there and see what we can see?'

Benjy was all for that, so off they went up the lane towards it.

It was a long walk. It took them an hour just to start climbing the hill. When they reached the top, they gazed down over the land beyond. In the distance they could make out a few houses clustered together. They made their way down towards them. As they got nearer, they realised one of the buildings was an inn.

'Let's go inside. I could do with a drink. I'm parched,' said grandfather.

There was a bald-headed man behind the bar, waiting for customers. His face brightened when he saw them enter.

'Good morning,' he said in greeting. 'And a fine morning it is.'

'It is indeed,' agreed grandfather. 'We're taking advantage of it to have a long walk.'

'Very wise,' said the man. 'No point in waiting till it's pouring with rain to do that.' He chuckled to show how amusing the thought was.

Grandfather ordered drinks for him and Benjy, and soon he was sipping his and Benjy was sucking his through a straw. When Benjy had quenched his thirst, he looked at the man.

'Are there any dragons round here?' he asked.

The man looked puzzled. 'Dragons? I've never seen any. What makes you think that?'

'Or buck-toothed ogres ten feet tall?'

'Buck-toothed – Oh, here we go again. People like you coming here and asking daft questions. Almost every day I get people calling in and asking about elephants with two trunks or horses with tusks. No, there are none – not that I'm aware of.'

'What about crocodiles without any teeth?' persisted Benjy.

'Or ostriches that jump about like kangaroos?' added grandfather.

The man glared at them. 'I think you're trying to make a fool of me. I'm not putting up with that. Finish your drinks and get out. I can do without customers like you, even if I don't earn a penny for the rest of my life.'

Surprised by the man's attitude, Benjy and his grandfather drank the rest of their drinks and left the inn. They started to walk away, but hadn't gone twenty yards before the man came out and shouted after them.

'Hey! Are you from that village over the hill?'

Grandfather confirmed that they were.

'Is it true that there's a cat there that always wear spectacles and has a white feather for a tail?' the man asked.

'Yes, it's mine,' said Benjy. 'My dad bought it for my birthday. He's saving up to get me a dog with a parrot's face – one that can talk.'

'Come on, Benjy,' his grandfather urged him. 'We'll have to get home before teatime to feed that cat of yours. You know his feather drops off if he doesn't eat regularly.'

It was all the encouragement Benjy needed. The last thing he wanted was a cat without a tail *or* a feather. So off they went at a brisk pace.

BOSSY BOOTS

Polly folded her arms fiercely. She glared and she pouted. It was a wonder she knew how to be so frightening. She was only seven. But woe betide anyone who argued with her. It wasn't only little girls of her own age who would feel the lash of her tongue. It was boys much older ... her teachers at school ... her parents!

Like now at the dinner table.

'I told you I don't like carrots. And I'm not having them, so scrape them off my plate or I'll throw them across the room again.'

She meant what she said. It wouldn't be the first time Polly had thrown anything across the room. Once she'd even broken a window when she'd hurled a new pair of shoes through it. She'd hated the buckles on them.

'But, Polly, carrots are good for –'

'I don't care, don't care, don't care!' shouted Polly, drowning out her mother. 'They're an ugly colour and make me sick.'

'I've never seen you be sick,' said her father, trying to tease her.

'Make me sick inside, stupid!' retorted Polly. 'Though I can be sick all over the floor as well, if you want.'

'No, no, that won't be necessary,' said her father, raising his hands in a calming manner.

With a sigh, her mother got up from her chair and swept the carrots from Polly's plate onto her own.

'No point in wasting them,' she said.

'I didn't say you could have them,' objected Polly. 'They were mine and I should say what happens to them.'

'Now, now, Polly. You're going too far,' said her father. 'We paid for them, so actually they belong to us. If your mummy wants –'

'She's not my *mummy*! I'm not a baby. Say "mum" or "mother". Or even Mrs Tweedy – which is a silly name, and I wish it wasn't mine. You should have changed it long ago. But you're too silly yourselves to have done it. No, don't eat those carrots … *Mummy*. Put them in the bin. You've got to put them in the bin.'

It wasn't very different at school. Polly soon put her foot down with the teacher if she wasn't making herself clear.

'How can I expect to learn anything if you're confusing me?' she'd complain.

Or: 'Do speak more slowly and stop gabbling.'

Naturally, this didn't go down well with the teacher, who wasn't prepared to let a little girl talk to her like that. So she tried to stop her – whereupon all the other children in the class started giggling. They knew it was a waste of time.

Then, one day, a new girl started at the school. She was only five, so it may have been the first school she'd attended. No one knew for sure; for when someone asked her, she told him to mind his own business. Then she told a group of children to get out of her way or she'd stamp on their toes.

It just so happened that Polly was among the group. She gawped in amazement at the girl – and was seen to be doing so by the girl.

'What are you staring at?' she demanded. 'Never seen a girl before? Have you not got a mirror at home? Or are you too scared to look at yourself in it because you're so ugly?' Having said which, she flounced away, leaving Polly flabbergasted.

The new girl's name was Amanda, and she was about to give her teacher as hard a time as Polly gave hers. When the teacher welcomed her to the class and introduced her to the other children, Amanda stressed that her name was Amanda, and if anyone called her Mandy, they'd regret it for the rest of their lives, as would any boys who tried to tease her, and any teacher who dared to shout at her. Having made her position clear, she allowed the teacher to proceed with the lesson.

The other children kept glancing at her, as if they couldn't believe that a girl of their age would talk like that to a teacher.

Or like that to her parents, because that's what she did all the time. Her father was a nervous man who hated arguments, so he tended to agree with everyone. More than once he'd found himself agreeing with both his daughter and his wife at the same time, even when they disagreed with each other – which they usually did. Naturally, Amanda thought her parents as silly as Polly thought hers were.

At lunchtime, Amanda went home for something to eat. It was only a short distance from the school and she refused to let anyone come to escort her. When she entered the house, her father was even more agitated than usual.

'Don't take your coat off, Amanda. We've got to get to the hospital. Your mum's been taken there. I'll get the car out.'

Amanda took her coat off. 'I want something to eat first.'

'When we get back. You can wait that –'

'I want something now. I'm hungry.'

'But –'

'I'm starving. And I'm not going in that old car. I want to go in a taxi.'

'A taxi? But why? Our car isn't that old.'

'I want something to eat and I want to go in a taxi, or I'm not going.' Amanda had started sulking. Not a good sign.

Her father knew it was pointless trying to change her mind, so he quickly made a couple of sandwiches – of the kind she liked – then phoned for a taxi. Miraculously, Amanda didn't make any more complaints and soon they were speeding off to the hospital.

Once they arrived, they were directed to the room where Amanda's mother was to be found. They entered, and there she was, lying in bed, with a cot beside it.

A cot with a baby inside.

Amanda's parents gave each other a kiss while she stared at the baby. Its eyes were half-closed and a streak of spit was dribbling from its mouth.

'This is your new sister,' Amanda's father said, proudly.

Amanda pulled her face. 'I didn't say I wanted a new sister. Whose idea was it?'

'She'll be someone you can play with when she gets older,' said her mother, smiling as though it was something to look forward to.

'I don't want anyone to play with. You should have asked me first. You're not bringing her to our house.'

'It's her house as well now,' her father pointed out.

That didn't go down very well with Amanda. She scowled and couldn't take her eyes off the baby. She still regarded it as an 'it' and not a 'her', and couldn't imagine ever wanting to play with it.

After her parents had exchanged a few more words, her father said he had to go.

'Better take Amanda back to school. I'll pop in again later,' he told his wife.

Amanda didn't say goodbye to her mother; she was too busy being angry. She and her father headed towards the door. As they reached it, they heard a voice they hadn't heard before.

'Oy, you two!'

They turned towards the bed. The baby was sitting up in her cot, glaring at them.

'Just make sure you switch the light off before you leave!' she snapped.

Or *it* snapped, depending on your point of view.

THE FRISKY DOG

There was nothing more that Topsy liked doing than running about on the beach. She was a Golden Labrador who loved splashing about in the shallow water at the sea's edge. She eagerly chased after the small ball thrown by her owner as far as he could. She would have liked it even more if he could have thrown it a long way. But he couldn't. He was an old man who had a bent back and trudged about with a stick to help him. And his arms ached. He could throw the ball only ten yards, which Topsy covered in two giant bounds. She would bring the ball back for the old man to throw again, which he did. But only another ten yards, which Topsy reached in two giant bounds again. In other words, it wasn't much fun.

But Topsy didn't mind too much. She raced about, chasing seagulls when they landed on the sand to look for food, even though she could never catch one. It wasn't certain that she wanted to.

There were never many people on this stretch of beach. But every now and then a boy and a girl came with their dog. They too ran about in high spirits. And they threw a ball a good distance, hoping that Jasper, their beagle, would chase after it, as dogs usually did. But Jasper didn't. He showed no desire to dash here and there after a ball, as if he couldn't see any sense in doing it. The two children urged him to 'Go get it, Jasper', but he paid no attention. He simply strolled about with his head bowed, waiting for the visit to the beach to come to an end so they'd go home and he could have a snooze on the rug in the living room.

He was like the old man in that respect. The old man had done his duty in taking Topsy for a walk, and he couldn't wait to get home to have a snooze in his armchair. One might have assumed that the old man and the beagle were suited to each other, just as the two children and Topsy were.

And that was what the old man and the two children did assume. It isn't known who made the suggestion but they agreed almost straight away to swap dogs. The old man would have Jasper, the two children would have Topsy.

Of course, the dogs were surprised when they found themselves being led away by their new owners. Surprised and puzzled, because they hadn't indicated they would like to be swapped. Nevertheless, being placid dogs by nature, they went along with it. They were well fed at both new homes, and were treated no worse than they had been where they previously lived.

And the next time they were taken to the beach, Topsy went careering here, there and everywhere, while Jasper plodded about at a snail's pace. Nothing had changed in that respect.

The two children were delighted to have a dog they could run about with, while the old man was happy enough to be able to trudge about with Jasper by his side.

At least, they were at first.

But after a while, the two children found it difficult to keep up with Topsy. They got exhausted trying to match her speed. Soon they slowed to a walk while she went bounding on. The old man, on the other hand, recalling how much pleasure Topsy got from dashing about, tried to encourage Jasper to do the same. He threw the ball and urged Jasper to chase it. But all Jasper did was trudge after it, pick the ball up in his mouth, then drop it again for the old man to throw again – if the old man really wanted to do it. Jasper himself hoped he wouldn't.

The old man did more than that. He started jogging to the ball very slowly to show Jasper how dogs normally behaved. He then picked up the ball and threw it again – this time, with a huge effort, all of twenty yards. Jasper looked after it, then started trudging towards it.

'Go get it, Jasper!' the old man cried. It was what the two children used to cry. And it had no more effect now than it did then. Jasper didn't increase his speed. In fact, the old man overtook him to get to the ball first. He was still using his walking stick but it seemed he'd at last learnt how to run. Scooping up the ball, he threw it thirty yards then ran after it himself, while Jasper kept trudging behind.

The two children, meanwhile, had given up chasing after Topsy. Occasionally they called her name to try to get her to come back, but that never worked when Topsy had a beach to explore. So they trudged about – just like Jasper – waiting for her to tire herself out. But she didn't. They got more tired of trudging than she did of running. Soon they were moving no faster than the old man used to do.

He was now scampering about faster and faster in a vain effort to persuade Jasper to do likewise. He ran after the ball, picked it up, threw it again and raced after it, hoping Jasper would try to beat him to it. Jasper never did. All the beagle did was watch the old man do what the two children did when he was their dog.

Something strange had happened which neither the dogs nor the old man nor the two children could quite understand.

It was puzzling. The old man was running about like a frisky dog. The two children were trudging about like a pair of old people.

Topsy and Jasper were amused. To see their former owners behaving in such an unusual fashion was like being tickled on the tummy. And when the old man started splashing about in the shallows like Topsy, they wanted to burst out laughing like humans. Some people, who were also on the beach that day, did start sniggering at the sight of the old man in the sea with his clothes on. Not wishing to give offence, they turned away so he wouldn't see them.

Actually, he was enjoying himself so much that he hardly noticed they were there. It was years since he'd been for a paddle in the sea. He'd forgotten how delightful it was – as long as he didn't get stung by a jelly fish, that is. He'd always been scared of that happening.

'Come on in,' he shouted to the children. 'It's not cold.'

The children had always liked paddling in the sea. They didn't care tuppence about jelly fish. But they didn't want to get their shoes and socks wet, so they took them off first and then joined the old man in the water.

Topsy, of course, was quick to jump in too. And Jasper ... well he trudged in. But, whether he admitted it or not, he enjoyed himself just as much as the others.

There's nothing quite as nice as a paddle in the sea.

THE SNEEZE

In a land as far away from one place as it was from another lived a boy who refused to wear a cap. It caused a lot of bother. His parent warned him every day that if he wasn't wearing one when it rained, he might catch a cold and be sneezing all the time. Other villagers too shook their heads in fear of what might happen.

'I remember a young man once who had the same idea,' said a wizened old woman. 'He started sneezing so hard he almost blew his head off. And all because he thought he knew better than the old folks.'

The boy, whose name was Herman, thought he knew better than everyone. It hadn't rained for months, and he couldn't see the sense of wearing a cap till it did. It never rained much in this part of the world. Farmers were often seen on their knees begging for a downpour so their crops would grow. But clouds hardly ever appeared, and when they did, they were usually very small and floated away without dropping any rain at all.

All the other children in the village followed their parents' advice and wore caps or bonnets they'd been given specially for the expected deluge. But Herman continued to play in the streets and fields bareheaded. In his shorts too, for that matter.

As the weeks passed, the old folks decided it was time to put raincoats on as well.

'When it comes, it'll be a heavy downpour for certain,' a bearded old man declared. 'No point in getting our shirts wet when we've all got raincoats.'

Naturally, Herman had no intention of wearing a raincoat. He couldn't play football in one of those. So although his parents pleaded with him, he dismissed them with a wave of his hand and went outside without it.

When another two weeks went by, the call came from elderly people to carry an umbrella about at all times.

'I've seen some who didn't bother and paid the price,' said one, opening out his umbrella and holding it above him. 'They were caught unawares and got wet through. One chap, I recall in particular, couldn't stop sneezing for a year. Whenever I had a conversation with him, he couldn't finish a sentence without sneezing halfway through it.'

For days the villagers – even the children – went about with umbrellas. Not Herman. He thought umbrellas were a nuisance. The only thing he liked carrying about was a football. Umbrellas weren't much use when it wasn't raining.

Nor were wellington boots, for that matter. But with the number of dry days increasing, it seemed certain to everyone that when the rain came, it would fall in torrents and leave lots of puddles on the ground. So everyone started wearing wellingtons. They didn't want their shoes ruined by getting soaked. Not Herman, of course. He found wellingtons cumbersome and wouldn't wear them at any price.

'Just wait till his feet are wet and cold,' someone muttered. 'It'll be too late then.'

And whoever said that was right. For when the rain eventually fell, as it did the following week, it *was* too late. Herman wasn't wearing wellingtons or a cap or a raincoat, and he wasn't holding an umbrella over his head. He stayed indoors most of the time till the rain stopped.   But he did start sneezing for some reason. He only sneezed once, mind … then never sneezed again. Never. Not in his entire life. However wet he got from rain or swimming, he couldn't manage another one. He tried and tried but he couldn't. He would have liked to sneeze at least once more. It was such an interesting thing to do.

    Don't you think so?

SWAPS

Mr and Mrs Clay lived with their little boy Reginald in a nice house by the seaside. They should have been happy but weren't. Mrs Clay was sick and tired of clearing up Reginald's toys after he'd finished playing with them. No matter how many times she told him to put them away neatly, he would just ignore her. She was ashamed that her house always looked untidy when anyone came to visit. In the end she couldn't take it any longer. So she swapped her little boy for a new rug. When she laid it out in the living room, it did look nice. Even Mr Clay agreed that she'd been very wise in her choice. For two days they sat in their armchairs gazing with satisfaction at the rug instead of watching television. It was a rug with a diamond pattern and a long pile.

That was the trouble. For first one mouse then another found the pile very comfortable to live in. Soon four or five of them were scurrying about all over the living room. Neither Mr Clay nor Mrs Clay liked mice, so they swapped the rug for a cricket bat. Mr Clay played cricket for a local team and needed a new bat as his other one was showing signs of wear. How proud he was when he walked out to the wicket with his new bat. And what a good bat it proved to be. For he hit the very first ball for six – right over the boundary. But it smashed a window in the vicar's house. The vicar insisted that Mr Clay pay for the repair, and since it was a lot of money for such a large window, Mr Clay didn't have enough savings to pay for it straight away. So he swapped the cricket bat for a posh vase and didn't play cricket again.

Mrs Clay put the vase on a small table, and it was such a pretty vase that she and Mr Clay sat in their armchairs gazing at it instead of watching television. The problem was that very often, when either of them went near the table, they bumped into it so that the vase wobbled and almost fell off. Frightened that if it got smashed they would lose something very valuable, they swapped it for a little girl named Marjorie. Mrs Clay insisted that little girls were much tidier than little boys and she wouldn't have to keep picking up toys. So Marjorie settled in and soon showed she was more interested in playing in the garden than with silly toys. The result was that she got very dirty. Her clothes were covered in soil, and no matter how many times Mrs Clay told her to stop rolling about on the grass, she just ignored her and kept doing it.

So Mrs Clay swapped her for a new washing machine. She needed it to get Marjorie's clothes clean again. Of course, once she'd got them clean, they didn't need to be washed again, since Marjorie wasn't there any more. And since she and Mr Clay always kept their clothes very clean, she knew she wouldn't have to wash those for a long time. So she swapped the washing machine for two bicycles. They'd decided to take up cycling as a hobby, and planned to ride out into the country for a picnic on a field somewhere. But no sooner had they set out than Mr Clay got a puncture and had to repair it. Then, when they set off again, Mrs Clay got a puncture and had to repair that. Then Mr Clay's brakes failed and he came a cropper in a ditch.

So they swapped the bicycles for a new wardrobe. Mrs Clay had so many clothes she needed another one to hang them all up. But how the doors creaked when she opened them. Even a drop of oil didn't stop them. So she swapped the wardrobe for a bottle of perfume. But a whiff of that made Mr Clay sneeze, so she had to swap that – very reluctantly – for a garden spade. The soil needed turning over before anything was planted, and Mr Clay enjoyed gardening.

This time, though, his back started aching, and eventually he had to stop before it seized up completely. So they swapped the spade – for Reginald. He was available again because he was just as untidy in his new home, and everyone there was fed up with him. It was nice to have Reginald back with them even if he did start making a mess again. They told him about all the swaps they'd made since they last saw him – the nice rug and the wardrobe, the little girl and the cricket bat, the bicycles and the washing machine, etc.

He was disgusted at their behaviour.

So he swapped them for a chocolate bar, which he scoffed all by himself.

Which meant he had nothing left to swap.

He shouldn't have been so greedy.

Printed in Dunstable, United Kingdom